To
Dad/Samuel,

Happy Christmas '97,

Lots of Love Always,

Paul & Shola.
xxxx

PROCLAIMED IN BLOOD

PROCLAIMED IN BLOOD

True Crimes Solved By Forensic Scientists

Hugh Miller

HEADLINE

First published in 1995
by HEADLINE BOOK PUBLISHING

10 9 8 7 6 5 4 3 2 1

British Library Cataloguing in Publication Data

Miller, Hugh
Proclaimed in Blood
I. Title
363.25

ISBN 0-7472-1171-X

Typeset by
Letterpart Limited, Reigate, Surrey

Printed and bound in Great Britain by
Mackays of Chatham PLC, Chatham, Kent

HEADLINE BOOK PUBLISHING
A division of Hodder Headline PLC
338 Euston Road
London NW1 3BH

To preserve anonymity, and to avoid causing distress or embarrassment to innocent people, certain names and places in the following case studies have been changed.

Contents

Acknowledgements

I am indebted to Lonnie James and Everett Power in Los Angeles, Dave Gort in Amsterdam, Dr Erich Walser in Berlin, and Professor Joe Temple, who seems to be everywhere. A number of other people who helped greatly have asked that I do not identify them. I have concurred, and I thank them warmly.

Special thanks to the owners of photographs who were happy to dig them out so that I could make my selection, and to the others, Janice, Eric and Gail in particular, who ran through miles of tape and shifted reams of paper to find testimony I could listen to and facts I could check.

Preface

Apart from being an intriguing and perhaps informative collection of cases from around the world, this book may be a timely reminder that forensic science, for all its publicised shortcomings, can often deliver the goods when other forms of investigation are stymied. More than once a wrong-shaped bloodstain, a hidden wound or a curious something under a fingernail has kick-started a case which has gone static on the police. More than once the men in white coats, not the detectives, have prevented some villain getting away with murder.

To be fair, it doesn't usually work that way. Most often forensic specialists will work alongside the police and add their measure to the structure of an investigation. Some of the cases here are in that category, and most of them concern murders. That is no accident. Murder is the quintessential, fascinating darkness of humankind, the worst in people; the investigation of it reveals forensic scientists at their best.

This, then, is a look at the work of the men and women who attack crime with the tools and the substantial cunning of forensic science. There are no dramatic embellishments. What the reader is meant to find is an engrossing selection of insider vignettes of crime from a number of perspectives. There is no attempt to make a study of forensic procedures or to offer a stiff-necked critique, since I am driven by a wish to impart, and little else. These are plain case descriptions, told as far as possible in the words of the people who were involved. They are enthralling.

Hugh Miller
Warwick, January 1995

Death of a Call-Girl

In the city of Glasgow in 1959, Vanessa Clyde was a true local rarity, a high-class prostitute. She had trained as a teacher and taught infant classes at a primary school in Rutherglen, on the outskirts of Glasgow, until 1957, when prostitution seems to have become her full-time occupation.

'She told me once she started on the game by accident,' said Dinah Lewis, a one-time psychiatric social worker who struck up an acquaintance with Vanessa at the time of her one and only scrape with the law. 'She was nineteen at the time, still a student, and she was short of money for food, for books and for the rent. She had a decent enough grant, but she gave far too much of it to her widowed father. He was a classic layabout, a really repulsive man with a beer belly, an imaginary heart condition and a daughter who believed the sun blazed outward from his wishbone.'

Vanessa complained about her miserable financial position to a friend, also a student, who lived at the same residence where Vanessa rented a room. The friend told her bluntly that if she really needed money and wasn't too finicky about how she earned it, there was a good regular income to be made on the Glasgow hotel-bar circuit.

'The other girl had been doing weekend soliciting for a year

1

or thereabouts,' Lewis said. 'It wasn't such an uncommon thing back in the fifties. A percentage of young women who were students, or were in the lower-paid professions, often went on the game. It was harder for them to pick up part-time jobs. Employment in general was still angled towards men, and when a woman could get a job the pay was usually terrible and always far less than a man would have been paid for doing the same work. Vanessa's friend said she picked up £10 for an evening's work, and that was an average wage because she had average looks. When she felt like it she would go out two or three nights on the trot and make enough to last her comfortably for weeks. She said Vanessa would be able to pick up a lot more, being a real blonde with a good, compact figure and looking so wholesome.'

Vanessa was not shocked by the suggestion, but she suspected the work was dangerous and did not take her friend's advice. But as time passed her financial position got worse, and a particularly unpleasant run-in with her bank manager – a meeting at which he took her chequebook from her and tore it in half – sent her back to her friend for details about how she could get into part-time prostitution.

'After her first time,' Lewis said, 'she thought she would never get over the shock of what she had made herself do with a complete stranger. Not that she was a virgin or anything like that, but her sexual experiences until that time had been very conventional, and she wasn't prepared for the untamed reaches of the hotel circuit. It took a lot of effort and real desperation to make her take that initial step, and afterwards she could scarcely believe she had gone through with it. It's funny how many girls say that, and then, before you know it, they've gone on to make their full-time living on the game.'

At that first encounter Vanessa let herself be picked up in an hotel bar by an anxious-looking man who stammered when he spoke and appeared almost as nervous as she was. He had a room in another hotel and on the way there in a taxi he sat at the opposite end of the seat from Vanessa and did not speak to her. 'That made her nervousness worse, the guy saying nothing, leaving a silence between them, a space for her to get anxious. She told me she nearly ran for it when they got out of the cab, but she kept reminding herself that she was poor, she was in debt, and for just a few minutes of misery she could erase a lot of the pain in her situation.

'When they got inside the customer's room he still didn't touch her. Instead, he had a couple of quick drinks of whisky, then told her what he wanted her to do. He didn't look at her when he told her, and when he had finished talking Vanessa was sure she was going to run away.'

In the end she did not leave until she had earned her money – £10 and a bonus of 10s for her taxi fare home. For fully three days afterwards she could not let her mind settle on what she had done, but by the end of the week a perspective developed, and with it came a sense of proportion. Vanessa realised she had earned very good money and had not engaged in anything she would have called sexual activity. Furthermore, she had pocketed a full 10 guineas freely given by a man who had not laid a finger on her at any time during the transaction.

'Finally she rationalised it,' Lewis said. 'That's usually what happens. She took the brightest view possible, which would ease her along towards doing it again. She told me she set the facts out plainly in her mind, so that she could weigh it all up logically, unemotionally, and see if in fact she had been harmed, or so upset or pained that she could not take that route again when she needed extra cash.

'To anyone on the game or on the psychiatric scene, even at that time, the transaction between Vanessa and the man was not very unusual. In fact it was tame, because she didn't even have to take off her clothes. All she did was kneel astride him as he lay on a rubber sheet and urinate on his face. Bizarre, especially to a girl who had never heard of such things before, but not all that traumatic as sexual deviations go.

'In the end, time did its usual work of levelling everything out, and Vanessa decided there had been damn-all to it, it was money for nothing. Her shock had sprung simply from the *newness* of the experience, from the unconventional nature of it. Beneath any capacity for flap she was a pragmatist, and she decided she could adapt to any novelty if the price was right.'

Lewis believed that after that moment of acceptance, Vanessa had decided – subconsciously, at least – what professional direction she would eventually take. Schoolteaching never exercised any grip on her enthusiasm, although she did appear to have a genuine talent as an educator. 'Any way she thought about it, prostitution was the cushiest work in the world. It paid better than any other jobs she could imagine herself getting. That first fee had been earned very simply and if anyone was sullied it was the client. Vanessa was unharmed, and she came away with the equivalent of a week's wages for a schoolteacher.'

Vanessa's one brush with the law occurred near the start of her career, when she was unwary enough to be caught by a piece of police entrapment set up at the request of an hotel management. Vanessa went to court and was simply fined, but she told Dinah Lewis she would never put herself in that humiliating position again. 'She told me she had paid so much attention to other aspects of the job that she had skimped on some tactics, like watching out for sneaky policemen.'

The other aspects of the job had included the cultivation of a clientele more interested in fetishes and minor perversions than in conventional sex: 'I try to concentrate on the ones who like me to do things to them rather than the other way round,' she told Lewis. The plan was to set up a list of regular clients, operate the list on an appointments system, and eventually to get to a point of steady trade that would make it unnecessary for her to solicit.

Apart from Dinah Lewis, Vanessa Clyde was not known to have any other confidantes, and after a year she severed contact with Lewis. What is known about Vanessa's life as a call-girl is therefore mostly superficial. Her records showed that she conducted her business in clients' homes, in their hotel rooms, or in an apartment she owned in the middle-class Byres Road district of Glasgow. She had no pimp and no police record apart from that one prosecution for soliciting. New customers were found through personal recommendations. Among Vanessa's highest-paying clients were three senior police officers (none of them connected with the Glasgow Police) and a prominent criminal defence barrister. Vanessa's full-time career as a prostitute is believed to have lasted little more than twenty-three months, from a week after her twenty-second birthday to a few days before she would have turned twenty-four.

Early on the morning of 15 February 1959, Vanessa's dead body was found in the back courtyard of a tenement block at the Gallowgate in central Glasgow. She was hanging on a metal fence, her armpit impaled on a spike. Her car, a new Rover 90, was parked two streets away.

Dr Peter Strachan, a retired lecturer in criminology now living at La Jolla, California, worked as a forensic pathologist in Glasgow at the time Vanessa Clyde was murdered. The procurator fiscal appointed Dr Strachan to perform a post-mortem examination of Vanessa's body.

'She had been battered to death,' he said. 'Bruising intensifies and spreads after death, and by the time I saw the body, which would have been approximately twelve hours after she died, her abdomen, arms and legs were covered in huge purple bruises, here and there almost black, and her abdomen was distended and pulpy, suggesting extensive internal injury.'

5

According to the post-mortem notes, superficial examination revealed that Vanessa's ribs were broken on both sides, her front teeth had been punched out, and the roots of several incisors were sticking through her gums and lips. Her jaw and the frontal bones of her skull were fractured; her head had been repeatedly banged against something solid (a brick wall, it transpired) and the hair was clotted with brain tissue.

A few hours after the body was removed to the city mortuary, Dr Strachan carried out a full Crown post-mortem examination. He found that Vanessa Clyde had sustained a ruptured liver, ruptured spleen, tearing of the bowel in three places, and fractures of six ribs. Repeated kicking had caused a broken rib to make a deep puncture wound in her left lung. Most of the facial bones were broken and a comminuted skull fracture had caused massive damage to the brain. Together with scraps of grass and particles of earth and clay, fragments of blackish, sticky tissue were removed from beneath two fingernails. At the time of the post-mortem the substance had no apparent significance, but the specimens were put in a phial and kept.

'The cause of Vanessa Clyde's death was a toss-up,' said Dr Strachan. 'Any of the major traumas could have been the one that killed her, and since they all happened in so short a space of time, and to no apparent pattern, it was impossible to plot a course of progressive damage. I certified the cause of death as multiple injuries. At some point during the battering, her heart just gave out.'

In view of Vanessa's profession, it was not possible to say if she had been sexually assaulted at the time she was murdered. At some point during the evening she had had sexual intercourse – semen was found on a pessary retrieved from her vagina, and immediate microscopic examination showed that it was relatively fresh. At that stage in the development of forensic science, it was not possible to obtain a DNA profile or even a blood grouping from the semen.

Detectives and technicians went to Vanessa's flat and searched it thoroughly. Among the items they removed for further examination were three notebooks listing the names of dozens of clients, with details of dates and how much they paid. A total of sixty-two men were named.

'It was a nightmare of an investigation,' Strachan recalled. 'The law had stumbled on the kind of call-girl who could unseat boards of management and maybe a town council or two. Probably none of her clients ever realised how potentially dangerous she was. There were some really big names in those notebooks, and I couldn't tell the police anything that would help shorten the list of prominent bods they would need to interview.

'I admit that in an oblique way I enjoyed imagining the squirming of Vanessa Clyde's former clients when they were confronted with their iniquities, but that didn't affect my diligence, I promise you. I really couldn't tell the police very much – they were looking for a man capable of battering a healthy young woman to death. Full stop. We didn't have one evidential shred or speck we could link to the killer, and there was nothing in his method, or lack of it, that told us much beyond the likelihood that he was strong and had a terrible temper.'

The drudgery and embarrassment of suspect elimination took weeks to complete. A number of the men who had to be interviewed were out of the country, others were reluctant to be seen, and several of those who were interviewed were so evasive that it took days to check their alibis. Sixteen days into the investigation, one of the men named in the notebooks committed suicide before the police had a chance to interview him. For a time it was thought he might be the murderer, but detectives eventually unearthed firm evidence which put him in Newcastle at the time Vanessa was killed. Twenty-four days after the murder the police had no suspects and no promising lines of inquiry. 'The case has produced surprisingly few clues, and no witnesses at all,' a press officer announced at the time.

'They were stumped,' Strachan said. 'It had reached the stage where they were beginning to see significance in the smallest and silliest things. So was I. One morning at half-past six I managed to get myself in such a state over the case that I went down to the mortuary, woke up the night attendant and got the body out of the freezer. I examined every inch under strong lights and came away as wise as I had gone in. Later that day, it dawned on me that I might gain something by having a look at the sticky tissue stuff I'd poked out from under the fingernails.'

The flexibility and sliminess of the fragments suggested that they could be human tissue, but the colour and the way in which they had begun to decompose was not typical. There was something unusual about the texture, too – something missing rather than a mysterious presence. 'It was hard to specify what was *not* human about the matter,' Strachan said. 'But when you've spent years getting the various strata of skin and other human tissue on your gloves and on the handles of your knives you develop a feel for it. This stuff from Vanessa's fingernails had some of the qualities, but others, difficult to specify, definitely were not there.'

Strachan soaked the black, semi-decomposed fragments in glycerine to make them more flexible, and to exclude oxygen, which would otherwise hasten the decomposition. Over a period of days the fragments flattened out and became pliable enough to be placed on two microscope slides. Strachan kept one specimen, no larger than a fly's wing, and sent the other to the Department of Histology at Glasgow Royal Infirmary. 'I was trying for some halfway decent scientific elimination,' he explained. 'I was sure the stuff wasn't animal, but I needed to have the certainty reached on a methodical basis, and I wanted some clue to point me in an investigative direction. Any dead-end chase would be better than sitting on my hands and thinking in circles.'

At the histology laboratory the tiny specimen was examined under various kinds of illumination in an effort to disclose some information about its structure. Viewed by short-wave light at an eighty-times magnification, the tissue could be seen to have a system of veins and capillaries, and when high-intensity light was passed directly through it, a red tint was clearly visible among the muddier colours of decomposition. 'It had us foxed, that stuff,' a retired histologist recalled. 'We suspected we were dealing with something pretty common, but without any clues beyond its own disintegrating structure, we were up a dark alley.'

There was not enough of the material for anything approaching a full analysis, but a partial chemical breakdown of a tiny fragment revealed that the tissue was probably vegetable in origin, and a few microscopic pollen molecules were visible in the fibres.

'As soon as I heard that, I made a rash guess,' Strachan said. 'I sent both slides to Denis Munro, a botanist in Edinburgh, a brilliant man who had helped the police a number of times when the provenance of plants and agricultural debris had been in question. I told him my guess and asked if he could confirm it or offer me an alternative. He was a man who loved a challenge and he promised to let me have an answer within twenty-four hours.'

In fact Munro was on the telephone to Strachan within twelve hours. He had looked at the slides at various magnifications and under various kinds of lighting, and what he saw had confirmed Strachan's hunch: the tissue was the decomposed remains of a flower petal.

'That was as far as Munro could take it. He couldn't say what kind of flower,' Strachan said. 'The decomposition was the

9

problem. The essential features were there, but so much else was corrupted that all he could say with certainty was that I had sent him fragments of a petal. So the revised position, from an investigative standpoint, was that we had the remains of a flower petal taken from beneath the fingernails of a murdered woman, and as far as we knew that was the only potential clue to who killed her. So I suppose we could claim we knew something more than we did a week before, but not enough to suggest an avenue of inquiry. I couldn't leave it there, could I?'

After some thought, Strachan telephoned a friend at an institute of tropical medicine in Paris and asked her advice. She suggested that he called Dr Thomas Hinton, a toxicologist in London. Hinton had established a photomicrographic library of thousands of plants and was in the process – a five-year task – of relating the plants and their component parts to various types and sub-types of vegetable poisons. Among these poisons were some which resulted directly from the processes of decomposition in certain plants.

Strachan called Hinton and he agreed to examine the specimens, but warned that it might take him some time to get around to looking at them. He added that Strachan should not rush him, since he hated being put under pressure and such behaviour would probably result in the specimens being sent back unexamined.

Strachan had to wait three weeks. In the meantime, Glasgow Police investigated the confession of a man who claimed to have known Vanessa Clyde for six months and to have killed her in a rage when she tried to demand extra money for her services. Nobody took the confession seriously but it had to be investigated, since it was technically a lead – indeed, it was the only one.

'Whatever Vanessa Clyde's shortcomings,' a retired police-woman recalled, 'she was fastidious in her choice of clients. She preferred men with intelligence, men equipped with a bit of social refinement, and definitely men who were scrupulous about their personal hygiene. The man who told us he had murdered her was a self-employed gas-fitter who didn't look as if he ever washed. He had a smell off him that one police officer said was worse than any gas leak. He was also illiterate, and he had previous convictions for gross indecency. A psychologist described him, off the record, as arguably sub-human.'

Dr Hinton finally returned the specimens to Glasgow. A brief note was enclosed:

> In spite of the fairly advanced degree of decomposition in the enclosed specimens, I can say with certainty that they are petal fragments of a light red bloom of *Dianthus caryophyllus*, the cultivated carnation.

'From there on,' Strachan said, 'the whole case came to life again. The police appealed for witnesses who might have seen somebody wearing a red carnation in the Gallowgate area on the night Vanessa Clyde was murdered. A man wearing a flower wasn't exactly a common sight in that district at any time.'

Within forty-eight hours the police had three reported sightings of a man wearing a red flower on the night in question, and two of them provided descriptions which coincided on major points: the man was tall, well built, well dressed, and he had a particularly noticeable nasal deformity.

Three days after the specimens were returned to Strachan, a fifty-two-year-old retail draper, Joseph Campbell, was picked up for questioning. Apart from fitting the physical description – he was tall, well dressed and had a disfiguring condition known as a deviating nasal septum – Campbell owned a shop near the spot where the body was found. He was also known to wear a flower in his buttonhole practically every day of the week.

At the police station the suspect put up a credible defence of bewildered innocence, but he could not give a satisfactory account of his movements on the night Vanessa Clyde died. A search warrant was obtained and Campbell's home was searched. Nothing incriminating was found. Then it was learned that he had an office on a quiet road in the Springburn district and another warrant was granted. Among a number of bank records and insurance documents, the officers found an envelope containing three pornographic Polaroid photographs of Campbell and Vanessa Clyde. Confronted with the pictures, Campbell confessed.

The story which emerged cast more light on the complex personality of the dead woman. Campbell, who lived in the affluent Kelvinside district of Glasgow, had a disturbed private life: in 1956 his son had committed suicide at the age of fourteen, his daughter was a chronic schizophrenic and his wife was an alcoholic. Campbell had been a client of Vanessa's for more than a year, and had been introduced to her by one of her other clients, a bookseller from Kilmarnock.

Campbell said that his relationship with Vanessa had been very special, and that during the time he had known her she had told him things about herself that she had never shared with anyone else. She admitted to him that in her sexual dealings with other men she had learned to subdue every trace of human feeling. It was a trick of detachment, she told him, and she had forced herself to learn it in order to keep the nature of her work from invading her mind at other times. While she never went into much detail about her other clients, she did say that what had begun as something simple and manageable had become complicated and sometimes frightening. Her greatest fear, she told Campbell, was that one day she might lose her mental discipline, and if that happened she was convinced she would go insane.

Campbell had a long-term arrangement with Vanessa for

which he paid an inflated rate. Every Saturday he visited his downmarket branch shop to check the books and collect bank receipts; on alternate Saturday nights Vanessa joined him at a flat he kept above the shop.

'The meetings were discreet,' Campbell told the police. 'Even my shop manager, who's been with me for more than twelve years, knew nothing about them.'

On the night Vanessa died, she and Campbell had argued. 'I'd been getting possessive, I suppose,' he said. 'She had turned into a bit of an obsession with me, one way and another. I didn't mean it to be like that, but what could I do? I wanted her to pack in that way of life. I said I wanted her to stop having other men, and I offered her money, regular money, as a substitute, so she wouldn't be out of pocket. But she said I was trying to tie her down, and she didn't want close attachments.'

When Vanessa left the flat that night Campbell followed her to her car, remonstrating with her, half angry, half pleading. Finally she told him she did not want to see him again.

'But I kept on at her, I'd had a couple of drinks and that makes me rant a bit anyway . . . I told her she was wrecking her life as well as mine and she should stop before it turned into a tragedy. But she wasn't going to budge, she just kept shaking her head.'

When Campbell offered to double the sum of money Vanessa grew angry. She shouted at him that she didn't want to see him again, not ever, and when he argued with that, she underscored the rejection by telling him he was a repulsive big bastard. 'I lost my head then. I started hitting her, just blindly, punching her for hurting me like that.'

Vanessa broke away from him. She ran along a passage beside a tenement and out into the courtyard at the back. He followed her, caught her and literally battered her to death. According to his statement, he remembered only catching her, then walking away from the body where it hung on the fence.

The record showed that Campbell had been in trouble with the police twice before. Once, when he was twenty-three, he had beaten and kicked a doorman after being refused entrance to a drinking-club where his membership had expired. The second time, two years before he met Vanessa Clyde, Campbell went to the home of an employee who had been caught pilfering. He beat the man so severely that he had to be detained for three weeks in the neurological unit at the Western Infirmary. A psychiatrist's note on the record said that in interview, Campbell displayed signs of serious neurotic disturbance: 'He is clearly unable to accept a secondary or submissive position in any situation where strong emotions are engaged.'

If the forensic pathologist, Dr Strachan, had not been so curious about the tiny sticky fragments he found beneath Vanessa Clyde's nails, Joseph Campbell would probably never have been caught. He was not named in any of Vanessa's notebooks, and all the clothes he had worn on the night he killed her, including his shoes, had been burned to ashes in the heating boiler at his home. He assured a police officer that if they hadn't found the Polaroids, he would never have admitted anything.

Charged with murder, Campbell was tried before a jury at the High Court in Glasgow on 12 October 1959. He was found guilty and sentenced to 20 years' imprisonment.

After serving ten years he was released from Barlinnie Prison on parole. He resumed control of his business, which had been run in his absence by his nephew. In 1972 at Portobello, a seaside resort near Edinburgh, Campbell attacked and seriously injured a newsvendor for allegedly short-changing him. A policeman appeared and Campbell ran off. Halfway across the road he was hit by a fast-moving coach and later died of his injuries in hospital.

Burning

It is rare for a crime scene to offer up only one worthwhile clue, and it's even rarer for the single clue to lead to the one piece of evidence that isolates the guilty party and puts him behind bars. But that was what happened when the Swedish police investigated a murder in a country district to the south of Uppsala, South-eastern Sweden, in the summer of 1983.

'It was the precise mid-point of the summer, and the papers made a lot of that,' said Inspector Erik Österling, who led the investigation. 'The general feeling among the mystics and other specially gifted people seemed to be that this death had an ominous occult significance. To us plain cops, it was just another murder.'

The victim was found in the early morning in a wood by a young forestry worker. In the centre of a clearing he came across a burned-out car. The hulk was still smoking and it was hot to touch. The worker saw what looked like a body slumped over the wheel.

The police were on the scene within the hour, bringing with them a couple of forensic scene-of-crime officers. They confirmed that the mass behind the wheel was a body. It was carefully dislodged from the wreck and transferred to the back of a van. 'An untrained eye couldn't tell from looking at it whether it was a burned roll of carpet, an old stunted tree or what the hell it was,' Österling said.

When the body had been removed the two forensic officers searched the roped-off area of the wood, a fifty-foot circle with the burned-out car at its centre. They worked slowly with great care, taking photographs and collecting specimens of ash and earth. As always at the scene of a crime, they were looking for anything leading backwards from the event to some clue that could be extended still further back, to reveal perhaps the outline of a motive.

'We found a print on the ground of a knife handle and part of the blade, nice and clear, and that was all that could be called good investigative evidence,' the senior forensic officer said. 'Later still, in the underbrush, we found some clothes, but the print of the knife remained the only potentially important find.'

There were no keys in the car. Back at the forensic lab the chassis was examined and a number was found which identified the vehicle. It was a two-year-old Citroën registered to someone called Anna Gullberg. Inspector Österling called at her address and Anna Gullberg answered the door herself. 'It was a shock, because I was ready to tell someone else that Anna Gullberg was probably dead,' Österling said. 'I changed tack quickly and asked if she was the registered owner of the car. She said she was, although her daughter usually drove it. The daughter, Selma, had not come home the previous night.'

Österling explained about the burned-out car and the body inside. He asked Anna Gullberg for a photograph of her daughter and the name of her dentist, since a jaw X-ray is a reliable guide when it is necessary to identify unrecognisable remains.

A leading forensic pathologist, Arthur Boye, was appointed to examine the body and to make comparisons between the dental X-ray plates and X-rays of the charred skull. 'There were a few structures where I could make comparisons,' he said. 'I could say with some certainty that the lower nasal area and the ramus of the jaw were similar enough to be certifiably the same. Several remaining fillings in the teeth corresponded to fillings on the dental record. The frontal sinuses were the same as on the skull X-rays, and to my reckoning that is as good as a fingerprint. Overall, I located twelve points of direct similarity between the two sets of X-rays, and that was enough to say that the charred body on my mortuary table was that of twenty-two-year-old Selma Gullberg.'

Later the same day, Boye performed a post-mortem on the body. Outwardly, as Österling had observed, there was little to indicate that the remains would be of much value to an investigator. However, it was clear that the body had been badly cut at the shoulders on either side of the neck, as if there had been an attempt at decapitation.

Locked in the moist cavity of the abdomen and chest, a number of structures can survive the ravages of a car fire. Boye found that the trachea was relatively intact, and he noted there was no staining by smoke at the upper or lower ends, and no particles of soot. That led him to assume, tentatively, that when the fire in the car started Selma was no longer breathing.

Boye worked on, moving steadily down the body, breaking away the outer shell to get at the leathery, roasted organs within. When he reached the vagina he found a wound beginning at the opening and extending six centimetres backwards and downwards through the tissue. 'It was a very deep wound,' he said. 'The vagina was filled with thick blood, the result of gravitational haemorrhage, perhaps exacerbated by the heat from the fire. I also noted that she was in the middle of her monthly menstrual period, although that had nothing to do with the type or quantity of blood in the vagina.'

Österling asked how the vaginal wound might have been caused, and the pathologist told him that from its clean,

17

straight appearance and the way the depth increased the further back it went, the weapon was probably a very sharp knife.

A vaginal smear revealed that no sperm cells were present, which could be taken as a firm indication that intercourse involving sperm release had not taken place. It was significant that no carbon monoxide was found in the blood. That practically confirmed that Selma had been dead when the fire started.

Österling had no illusions about their position. 'This was a sex crime, and the victim's name was Selma Gullberg. I was pretty sure of the first part of that, and completely sure of the second part. I could be certain of nothing else. I suggested we start investigating Selma's movements on the evening before she died.'

A few of the dead girl's friends were interviewed and eventually it was established that she had spent the hours between nine and midnight at a party in a house owned by the son of the local mayor. 'I make a practice of forgetting faces,' he told the police when they called. 'Maybe the girl you're talking about was with the student contingent that got here at nine and vanished around twelve. If people say she was here then I accept that, but I can't tell you anything about her or her movements.'

The house-owner's girlfriend was more helpful. She knew Selma and told the police that she had left the party around midnight with her friend, Carla Glas, and a young man called Per Moberg. She said Moberg could be found at the near-by tyre retread factory, where he worked as a labourer.

Österling and a couple of other officers went to the factory to speak to Moberg. He was tall and ruggedly good-looking, with long fair hair and a stubbly beard which looked carefully tended. 'I had the impression of a moody, sullen young man, well aware of himself, very self-admiring, too,' said Österling.

'You got the feeling that if he were made of chocolate he would eat himself.'

Moberg was working in a smoke-filled shed when the police showed up. He stayed there and carried on working while they questioned him, throwing chunks of rubber compound into a huge melting-pot. When he was asked if he knew Selma Gullberg, he freely admitted that he had spent time with her the previous night, volunteering the information that he had left the party with Selma and her friend Carla. 'Selma gave me a lift back to my flat in her car,' he added.

'Did she just drive you home,' Österling asked bluntly, 'or did you stop anywhere on the way?'

Moberg shrugged. 'Maybe we cuddled and messed around, you know? Nothing serious . . .'

'And then what?'

'I went in and listened to some music on my Walkman while I did a little ironing – when you're a bachelor you have to do that kind of thing, unless you're the kind that stays at home with Momma. Anyway, when I'd had enough of the ironing I went to bed. Selma didn't stay here, if that's what you mean. Why are you asking me all this, anyway?'

Österling told Moberg to stop working. It was time to have a look in his flat. Moberg tried to object, but the policeman warned him quietly that it would be pointless to resist the forward movement of an investigation, and if he persisted it would only make matters worse. So Moberg shrugged and complied. They got in the car and drove across town to his flat.

In the meantime Selma's friend Carla Glas was being interviewed at the hairdressing salon where she worked. She was told that Selma was dead, and when she had recovered sufficiently from the shock, the police officer suggested that it might have been Per Moberg who had killed Selma. Carla thought that was ridiculous. 'He wouldn't be able to do something like that,' she said. 'Anyway, I would have known if

Selma had been close to him, or if anything at all was going on between them. I've been close to her for donkey's years. We told each other everything. I mean that – everything.'

'Even about close personal relationships?' the police officer asked.

'Yes.'

'And did Selma have relationships with many men?'

'No more than most girls her age with her looks.'

The officer did not want to upset Carla any more than he could avoid, so he did not press her for a list of Selma's menfriends at that point. Instead, he asked if she could think of any man Selma had known who might have been capable of killing her.

'No, I can't imagine anyone . . .' Carla looked thoughtful, then said, 'Of course, she went around with Stig Ahlin for a while last year, quite a few months, I suppose.'

'What's he like?'

'He's a pig,' Carla said. 'Real pain in the backside. She finally packed it in with him when the money no longer made up for his lack of style. It took her a long time to get sick of him, but when she did it was over quickly. He still tried to make it up with her, though, even when she told him there was no chance of them getting together again.' Carla frowned. 'He was at it again only yesterday.'

Back at Per Moberg's flat, the police were searching the small bedroom he shared with another labourer from the factory. In a plastic rubbish bag by the door they found a freshly washed pair of blue socks. They were wet, and there were stains on them that looked like blood. Shortly afterwards an officer found traces of blood in the lavatory, too.

Österling asked Moberg why he had thrown away a perfectly good pair of socks – especially after having gone to the trouble of washing them.

'I just decided to dump them,' Moberg said, shrugging,

looking bored with the proceedings. 'I couldn't get them properly clean.'

'You mean the blood wouldn't come out?'

'It's not blood.'

'What is it, then?'

'No idea. But it's not blood. Couldn't be, I've been nowhere near blood.'

Österling decided it was time to get confrontational with Moberg. 'Let's stop messing around,' he said. 'My colleagues are searching this place very thoroughly, and if there's anything hidden they'll find it. Soon now they'll be in a position to say for certain that it's blood on those socks, and it's just like the blood in the lavatory. You've slipped up twice we know about, so the chances are there will be more little blunders. Why don't you just short-cut the whole situation and admit everything?'

Moberg blinked slowly. 'What am I supposed to admit?'

'There are traces of blood on your clothes and in the toilet,' Österling said. 'In addition to that, you were doing your washing at the dead of night, which is extremely suspicious.'

'Not for a bachelor. I was ironing too, remember? I just forgot to tell you about the washing. It slipped my mind.'

'You're just not convincing, Moberg. Why not stop trying to be smart and get honest for a change? It might be easier.'

Moberg asked Österling what made him think that the stains on his socks were blood.

Österling decided to cut the interview short. 'Mr Moberg, Selma Gullberg was murdered last night. You were the last person to be seen with her. I'm taking you into temporary custody for further questioning.'

Following the testimony given by Selma's friend Carla Glas, a few straightforward inquiries soon cleared Selma's former boyfriend, Stig Ahlin, of any suspicion. He had spent the whole night in the company of friends; all of them, interviewed separately, gave the same details of how Stig spent the night, right up until two-thirty in the morning, when they all turned in. Stig had slept on the floor with three others.

A forensic team moved in on Per Moberg's flat and made a thorough sweep. They took bagloads of clothing and other material back to the laboratory for examination. Moberg was asked to submit to blood sampling, and a complicating factor became apparent: his blood was group O, the same as Selma Gullberg's and, for that matter, the same as nearly half of the population, so it would be impossible to narrow down the identification of traces in Moberg's home to prove they had come from any person other than Moberg himself. A forensic haematologist explained that even the task of grouping the specimens was not straightforward.

'We had to verify the group indirectly,' she said. 'This is necessary when the cells have undergone dehydration, which often happens with small samples of blood. A sample from the window ledge in Moberg's flat looked like group O, but that was as close as we could put it – the sample was *like* group O. Microchemical tests were carried out on fluid from the lavatory and from the waste pipe of the bath, and it tested positive for blood, but there wasn't enough of it to get a grouping.'

Stains on Moberg's leather jacket were identified as human blood, but it was impossible to identify the group because under grouping tests certain enzyme-bearing materials in leather show properties like those in group B, frustrating any attempts at accurate grouping. 'It was all very confusing,' the haematologist said. 'Some cases are like that, they're full of complications, and yet others, often big and very important cases, are almost too straightforward to be true. The Moberg case was a swine, though. There was a T-shirt of his that had a clear bloodstain on it, and it gave a positive test as group B, but then it was suspected that the shirt had come into contact with the leather jacket, so the sample was not reliable and the careful, time-burning test had to be entirely scrapped.'

A pair of jeans showed signs of having been worn recently but there were few clues of any significance, beyond pine and spruce needles sticking in the turned-up bottoms of the legs. These were compared with similar debris from the clearing where the body was found, but the best the scientists could say was that they could have come from the same place. There were no distinct features to link the needles with any particular spot. 'And those socks,' the haematologist said, 'they were a real disappointment. Everybody was expecting them to give a strongly positive reaction for blood, but the stains turned out to be ground-in traces of asphalt.'

Inspector Österling and his team were sure Moberg was the killer, but their certainty was useless alongside the pitiful lack of hard evidence. 'The tests carried out so far were simply not adequate in terms of concrete proof,' Österling said. 'There was a lot of casting about for ideas, and my sergeant decided it would be a good idea to talk to Moberg's flat-mate.'

The flat-mate, who was called Tore Vesaas, had already been questioned. He confirmed the time Moberg had gone out on the night in question and roughly when he came back. He added that Moberg made a lot more noise than usual when he returned that night and seemed to be very agitated. The feeling about this witness was that he hadn't been able to tell the police very much. Österling's sergeant suggested that this was possibly because he hadn't been asked the right questions.

At his second interview Vesaas was asked what Moberg had been wearing when he went out on the night in question. This was already a matter of record, but Österling simply wanted a starting point that might lead the questioning somewhere unexpected.

'He had on his leather jacket,' Vesaas said, 'jeans, and white trainers and the knife, of course, slung on the belt.'

'Knife?'

'It's a decorative thing, he sometimes carries it for show.'

This had not been mentioned by anyone else. It was significant that the only unusual clue found at the scene of the crime was the imprint of a knife on the ground.

'You're sure about the knife?' Österling said.

'Definitely. It's not the kind of thing you forget – to be honest, it looks silly, because it's way too ornate, and it looks old-fashioned. But he likes it.'

There was no sign of a knife among Moberg's property. Suddenly it seemed that, in the absence of other evidence, the weapon might be crucial in forming the basis of a case against him. Österling took away a photograph of Moberg holding the knife and compared it to the cast of the imprint found by the burned-out car. The design was a match, as far as he could tell.

He went back to the prison and decided to have what he called a 'pressure session' with Moberg.

'Do you have a problem with the sight of blood?' Österling asked the prisoner.

Moberg said he had. Who had told Österling that?

'One of your friends.' It had been Vesaas. 'He told us you once ran out of a horror film because the sight of all the blood was making you ill.'

Moberg agreed that was true. 'But I didn't actually run. I walked away smartly, as I remember.'

'But is it true?' Österling stared at him. 'Can you stand the sight of blood, or can't you?'

'It depends,' Moberg said.

'Was Selma Gullberg having a period?'

'No.'

'How do you know that?'

'Well . . .' Moberg's eyes faltered, the first time Österling had seen that happen. 'I'd have got blood all over me.'

'So you had sex with her?'

'Yes.'

'Why didn't you tell me you were carrying a knife that night?'

Moberg made a show of trying to remember, then said he had forgotten. 'It wasn't important. It's more like jewellery, something for show, that's all. Anyway, I lost it, some time early in the evening.'

'You didn't have it with you in the car?'

'No, it'd gone by then.'

'What if I tell you that I know what the knife looks like, and that it's a match for the impression of a knife we found trodden into the ground at the place where Selma died?'

'I'd say that's nonsense,' Moberg said.

'What happened? Did you drop it as you jumped out of the car? Was it so slippery with blood that it slid out of your fingers? Is that what happened?'

Moberg began to look upset, but he visibly forced himself to remain calm. He told Österling he had nothing further to say.

'But you did use the knife on that girl, didn't you?'

Moberg stuck to his silent denial. It was clear now that if a case was ever going to be made against him, the knife would have to be found.

Since the beginning of the investigation the police had been trying to find the keys to Selma Gullberg's car, and against all hopes a diver finally found them in a river on the outskirts of town. The keys were lying on the riverbed at a point near a bridge almost midway between the small block of flats where Moberg lived and the wood where the murder had been committed. A forensic team visited the site and collected samples. Shortly afterwards Österling went back to the prison and presented Moberg with a scenario.

'You left the party with Selma Gullberg at around midnight. That has been confirmed. You set off in her car and the pair of you drove for about twenty minutes, then turned off along a track which took you to the place in the wood where the crime took place. Once you were there you wanted to have inter-course with Selma, but she had her period, or didn't want to.

25

You lost your temper and you attacked her and killed her.'
Moberg shook his head all the time Österling spoke.

'She was bleeding,' Österling went on. 'You lost your head and you started stabbing and mutilating her. Next you set fire to the car, dropping your knife in the process. Then you picked it up again and you ran away.'

Moberg continued to shake his head.

'While you were crossing the bridge over the river you realised you had Selma's keys in your pocket. You threw them into the water.'

'No!' Moberg suddenly shouted. 'You are wrong! I had nothing to do with that girl's death!'

'We know you threw your knife into the river, too. And then there are the particles of dirt and asphalt on your socks . . .'

'I told you they were dirty.'

'The dirt came from the area around the bridge across the river,' Österling said. 'There is fresh asphalt there and it stuck to the side of the bridge, and you got some on your socks because the legs of your jeans were turned up at the bottom. You were trying to get rid of the traces.'

Shouting again, Moberg insisted that it was just not true.

'Yes it is,' Österling demurred. 'You were trying to get rid of the blood on your clothes, too. Our scientists found conclusive evidence of blood on your clothes and in your toilet and in the waste trap of your bath.'

Moberg said that that was impossible.

Österling leaned close and spoke quietly and firmly. 'Apart from the knife, we have all the proof we need. You can be assured that we *will* find the knife, even if it means we have to dredge the river.'

An hour later Österling and his sergeant stood on the bridge over the river. The inspector had brought a mock-up of the knife he believed had been used on the night of the murder. The sergeant had already bet him that the knife would not float. Österling said it would, because the handle and the upper portion of the blade were hollow. He extended his arm out over the water and let the knife fall. It hit the water with an impressive splash and sank from view. The men moved to the other side of the bridge and watched the river flow away from them. A few seconds later the knife bobbed to the surface, several metres downstream. The sergeant handed over the money he had gambled.

Working on the theory that if Moberg had thrown his knife in the river it might have become lodged on a bank or in a weir, the police made inquiries at isolated houses, farms and small communities all along the downstream stretch of the river beyond the bridge. Eventually a dredger operator, Tarjei Jacobsen, who worked several kilometres from the bridge, was able to provide positive information. He had seen a flashy-looking knife floating downstream and he had fished it out.

'When I'd cleaned it up it was in excellent condition,' he told Österling. 'I wrapped it in newspaper and put it by the woodshed.'

Österling was delighted. He asked to see the knife and Jacobsen went to get it. But it was not where he had left it. After some confusion, it turned out that Jacobsen's wife had thrown it out with the rubbish.

Österling was devastated. There was nothing for it but to set off with his sergeant to the county incineration plant. Trying to find a solitary knife, however gaudy, among mountains of garbage seemed to both of them like a doomed venture. 'Our colleagues thought we had gone off our heads,' the sergeant said. 'And then to top everything, it turned out that we were on the wrong track anyway. On the day in question the plant had been out of action. The rubbish with the knife in it had been taken to another dump.'

The search took days. Dozens of police officers sifted steep piles of stinking rubbish, assisted by Österling, his sergeant and

Tarjei Jacobsen, who felt largely responsible for all the trouble they were having. Time after time knives and bits of knives were unearthed, some of them resembling at first glance the item they were looking for. Closer scrutiny would reveal that the similarities were only minimal and the search would continue.

Then an especially grimy specimen was turned up, sticking halfway out of a wad of filth-soaked paper. Even though it was in a terrible state, it did indeed look like the knife they were after.

Hopes ran high as the dirt was wiped off. Layers of slime and thick dirt were swabbed away from the blade, and as the inscribed pattern gradually emerged the sergeant became certain that it was the knife they were looking for. Then, as they examined the handle closely to identify the make, Öster-ling thumbed a lump of mud away from the top edge of the blade. A line of fine engraving was revealed. They examined it closely and made out the words: PROPERTY OF PER MOBERG.

The knife was taken back to the laboratory. The handle and blade were compared with the plaster impression taken at the scene of the murder. The patterns were identical.

From that moment on, making a case against Moberg was a routine procedure. A woman at the local hardware store even remembered him buying the knife, and paying extra to have it sent away to be engraved.

Although Per Moberg continued to deny that he had any-thing to do with the death of Selma Gullberg, he was found guilty of murder and sentenced to fifteen years' imprisonment.

Hyperkill

At first light on Sunday 7 October 1990, Louise Kaplan, a
thirty-four-year-old fashion photographer, was found dead in
an alley between two hotels in central Manhattan. Her body
was wedged among trashcans, her legs folded and her head
pushed down between her knees. The man who found the
body, a buildings inspector making a spot-check on a fire
escape, said he had noticed Louise only when he had climbed
on to a broken-down gurney to get a closer look at the
descender mechanism of the fire escape.

'After the shock, I couldn't help thinking how sad it looked,
that fragile girl in her nice clothes, bedraggled with the rain,
bundled between the filthy cans, her little white hands sticking
out like she was pleading to be seen.'

The comments of medical examiner Dr Buford Hamill were
less lyrical. He spoke into a tape machine when Louise's body
had been laid out for examination on a table at the morgue.

'The body of a young woman, early to mid-thirties, dressed
in a grey linen suit and black outer coat, both heavily soiled
with mud and animal excrement. There are scratches on the
deceased's face, on her neck and on the backs of her knees,
suggesting that she was attacked by someone with longish
sharp nails. Marked facial congestion, scratches around the

sides of the neck and the deep impression made by a yellow metal necklace, which is still in place, on the skin of the neck, probably caused by encircling hands, which have produced irregular bruising at the throat and the sides of the neck.

'The deceased is wearing no lower underwear and there are superficial signs of forced sexual intercourse – scratches again around the vulva and on the thighs, and what would appear to be a copious amount of semen in the pubic hair and around the entrance to the vagina.'

Louise Kaplan was the third young woman to have been raped and strangled in that part of Manhattan during a twenty-three day period. An appeal for information about her movements immediately prior to her murder produced practically no response. No one around the area where she died even recalled seeing her there.

Louise's secretary had been with her on the Saturday evening, when they attended an hotel reception for a visiting French couturier. They had parted company outside the hotel at a little after midnight; the secretary took a cab back to her apartment in Queens and Louise walked off towards a spot 200 yards away where her car was parked in a side street. That was probably the last time she was seen alive by anyone who knew her.

The car was found where it had been parked on the Sunday afternoon. It was unlocked, but it did not appear to have been vandalised. The police discovered evidence of a struggle inside. 'It was one of those nothing-too-obvious scenarios,' said Lieutenant Andrew Marsh, the officer leading the investigation. 'You look into a car, not expecting anything special, and you sense something wrong, but you can't see what. Then it dawns on you there are just lots of small things out of whack, nothing big, but added up they mean something important.'

The rear-view mirror was twisted too far to the side, so that it reflected the view through the front passenger window.

There were broad, arch-shaped smudges on the inside of the windshield which Marsh had to study for a while before they made sense to him.

'Knees,' he said. 'Louise had most likely been grabbed from behind as she slid in behind the steering wheel, and the reaction in a situation like that is that the whole of the body below the point of pinning – which usually occurs around the neck – lurches forward and uses its weight and its thrust capability to get the hell away from whatever is hanging on like that. This car was a sports model, so it was compact; the distance between the seat and the windshield wasn't much, so it was likely her knees would have hit the window and slid from side to side as she struggled.'

The neck restraint on the driver's seat was higher at one side than the other, further suggesting a struggle, and there were two notebooks and a pen on the floor by the transmission tunnel. 'Even the pile of the seat showed there had been a struggle,' Marsh said. 'It was a dark blue velvety material, and on the driver's seat it was all churned up, like somebody had spun something round and round on it. It wasn't a bit like the smooth, regular, grooved pattern you get from someone just sitting down.'

The back seat was marked, too, but only along the front edge, which suggested to the police that the assailant had been sitting on the edge, bent low, waiting for his victim. They also found a strange mark, a cluster of pinpricks in the interior padding in the rear arch of the car roof. 'I have to say we didn't pay too much attention to that,' Marsh said, 'but Doc Hamill did get interested in it, and it's a good thing he did.'

The murder had not taken place in the car. It happened fifty yards away in a dingy alley where Louise probably ran to escape her attacker. At the site where her body had been forced down between the trashcans there was further evidence of a violent struggle.

'She didn't make it easy for the bastard,' Marsh said. 'She was young and strong and I'd say she was a fighter, because a lot of women with similar build and capability just fold when they're attacked. Fear, mostly – sheer paralysing terror. But this lady fought back. At the back of your mind in a case like this, when a young woman has been put through this purgatory, and when you see that there has been a fight, you get this fervent hope she put the sonofabitch's eye out and he's holed up somewhere, suffering . . .'

A forensic team sealed off the alley where Louise had died. Over a period of eight hours every piece of rain-soaked debris was collected, its position was marked on a grid of the area, then it was bagged, labelled and sent to the laboratory.

'The lab was under pressure to get a linking factor on these rapes,' Marsh said. 'The killer's MO [*modus operandi*] was the same, more or less – there was a lot of scratching on the victims and it stuck roughly to a pattern. All three women were strangled, and the DNA profiling on the semen samples from the first and second victims proved that it was from the same person.

'But the trouble with that was it didn't tell us who he was. It didn't even point in his direction. That kind of evidence is great for corroboration, but in investigative terms it's nothing. We wanted a lead on the rapist. Something like a fingerprint would have been a lead to chase, but so far this prick had been lucky, the few prints he left behind were too badly smudged to be of any use. To tell the truth, even a carelessly dropped book of matches would have helped. The way things were, we didn't have a direction to run in. We were still blundering around all over the place and bumping into one another.'

DNA profiling of the semen from Louise's body did not work. The scientists were not particularly surprised. 'The sample had become badly degraded,' a technician explained, 'and it wasn't possible to produce a test result that would have any credibility in law. It was one of those things that happen.

Something in the victim's body chemistry worked rapidly on the components of the semen and broke it down to a point where it was useless for analysis.'

Within two years of this case, a degraded sample for DNA testing would not have been as much of an obstacle, because the sensitivity of the analysing equipment radically improved. But there in New York in October 1990 the forensic scientists were confronted with an impasse: three rapes looked identical, but with one of them they could not produce a DNA profile of the guilty party as a clincher.

Marsh was not prepared to believe that Louise had been murdered by somebody other than the man who had killed the other two women, but he had to admit the outside possibility of a copycat killing. 'You begin to get neurotic about these outside possibilities. Well, I do, and I know a lot of other people are the same. The way I saw it, the department hadn't given away much info about the MO of the killings, not officially. But somebody in the NYPD working on the case could have said something he shouldn't, or maybe somebody in the DA's office or on the medical examiner's staff could have said something – you know, being flashy with their inside knowledge – and just maybe some freak picked it up and used it to do a copycat killing.'

Being aware of such a possibility, Marsh insisted, a busy homicide detective's imagination can get out of control. His subordinate, Sergeant Louis Gordon, saw additional dark possibilities. 'A press guy could have stolen a peek at the records and let something slip,' he said, 'or he could even have committed the crime himself. Just like a cop could have. When you think about it, privileged though it was, that information could easily fall into the hands of any one of several hundred individuals.'

Marsh reluctantly agreed. 'It wasn't likely, but we had to keep the bad possibilities in mind. Any way you looked at it, this development with the degraded semen was not cheerful news.'

The investigative picture began to brighten a few days later, however, and it was as much a surprise to the forensic science team as it was for the police. Because of the rain on the night Louise Kaplan died, most of the debris taken back to the laboratory for examination had been soaked to the point where it was very unlikely that residual clues would be found. Nevertheless, everything was checked, and there was one unexpected find – a paper handkerchief. It had been crushed and discarded on the ground behind the body, where it was protected from the rain by a projecting brick ledge a few inches off the ground. The tissue had remained almost completely dry, and when a technician opened it carefully it was found to contain the kind of material that tends to excite forensic scientists.

'It was a yellow stain,' a senior technician explained, 'and when we examined it under the microscope it looked as if it was probably nasal in origin. There was mucus and large clumps of leukocytes – white blood cells. Well, the specimen was ideal for DNA profiling, because of the large amount of nuclear material.' Leukocytes have a nucleus – which in this context means a large component of the cell containing the genetic material – and so the nucleus, or a group of them, could be subjected to analysis which might yield a clear genetic profile of the person who had deposited the cells in the paper tissue.

'It was still not a fingerprint we could check against records,' Marsh said, 'but I could see why they were glad to find that tissue. With this specimen they hoped to win back some ground.'

A DNA profile was made using the material from the paper tissue, and it matched that made from semen in the first two murders. 'I think it was the sense of being rescued that energised me,' Dr Hamill said. 'I suddenly found myself thinking differently about these murders. It occurred to me that we should try looking at the less obvious clues – it had worked with a paper tissue, so why not with other evidential debris?'

Stepping aside from his medical brief, Dr Hamill obtained permission to examine Louise's car. He went equipped with suction collection apparatus, low-tack tape for picking up hairs and fibres, a macro camera for close-up photographs and a dust-mark lifting kit. A forensic team had already been through the car, but Hamill was convinced there was still more to be found. He admitted, privately, that at the time he had only his enthusiasm as justification. Fortunately, no one demanded any more than that.

'Straight away I got three good footprints from the back of the car,' Hamill said. 'I used the lifting kit, which electrostatically charges a sheet of plastic which then lifts indistinct footprints cleanly from a surface, so they can be examined away from their background and photographed clearly. Two of the prints turned out to be from the paper shoes worn by the forensic boys – those shoes *do* leave impressions when the foot is warm enough – but the third print was that of a stranger. It was ribbed, a fairly unusual pattern, and, mercifully, it was very clear.'

The shoe print was sent to the photographic lab to be copied and distributed to the various investigative divisions of the New York Police Department. In the meantime, Hamill was taking other photographs, concentrating on the curious arrangement of pinpricks in the rear roof-arch padding.

'I took ten shots, all instant pictures, and laid them out on the dash to dry. When they were ready I had my assistant take them to the senior officers on certain teams – homicide, robbery, burglary and so on – and get them to stare at the arrangement of pinholes to see what it suggested to them. I was prepared for this to be nothing, to be some kind of trauma to the car's lining that had nothing to do with the crime. I was ready for that, but I was hoping like hell it was more significant, and that somebody could see what the significance was.'

Shortly after Hamill had finished working on the car, word came back from a burglary unit that the shoe print tallied exactly with one they had lifted at the scene of a liquor-store hold-up two weeks before. An investigation was well underway. On the basis of security video pictures, three suspects were being sought and arrests were imminent.

In spite of the fact that several forensic technicians had been through Louise Kaplan's car, Hamill also turned up fresh evidence in the form of hair and fibre samples. 'Behind my back, some people were accusing me of being picky,' he said, 'because I was really digging down into crevices for my samples. The argument was that fresh evidence is all on the surface, or most of it is. But I know from experience that evidence from an area of violent struggle, especially when it happens in a tight space, can be found anywhere in the vicinity, from right on the surface to way down deep in upholstery and any other spaces there happen to be.'

The fibres were examined by low-power microscopy and were found to be a mixture of wool and polyester, dyed dark blue, a blend often found in certain brands of overalls and uniforms. Fibres found among other debris at the first two murders were compared and found to be identical, but for the moment the similarities were discounted, as the prevailing belief was that the fibres were too commonplace to have special significance.

The hair – only two strands were found – was dark and twisted spirally. When it was cut and examined under a microscope the section was found to be flattened and elliptical. 'It was Negro head hair,' said Hamill. 'When I made the announcement that we might just be looking for a black man, I may have sounded a little bit triumphant about the discovery, and there was some suppressed sniggering here and there, because the three suspects being sought in the liquor-store robbery were all black. I think the general feeling was that I had got lucky with the shoe print, but the rest was amateur time-wasting.'

Feedback was slow on the photographs of the pinprick marks on the car's roof lining, and when it did come it was half-hearted. In two instances the dots had been joined up with ballpoint pen to make silly faces; a third and fourth officer believed it was some kind of insect infestation. The fifth response, which came two days after the others, was more serious. An officer said he had seen the same effect before, and although he did not believe the pattern was the same, he was reasonably confident that the cause was identical.

'He said it was the imprint of a badge,' Hamill said. 'A badge with points and sharp facets, a showy kind of badge, like some security outfits issue to their employees.'

That possibility triggered another. The badge mark could have come from the hat of a security man who had left fibres of his uniform behind on the upholstery of Louise Kaplan's car. 'I got a serious analysis done on the fibres,' Hamill said, 'and we came up with the probable percentage of wool to polyester, and a spectrographic identification on the blue dye used on the material.'

The information was put together and cloth manufacturers were contacted. This took much less time that it would have done a few years earlier, because it was now the practice of most fabric manufacturers to keep detailed computer records of the make-up of their various lines. A computer asked to find a specific combination of wool, polyester and dye would find an answer – if there was one to find – a lot faster than any human being.

Hamill said: 'We got a hit within two days. A bulk fabric

manufacturer in the Bronx came up with the right stuff, plus a list of the people they sold it to, which happened to be only three companies, all of them in New York.'

By now, all three suspects in the liquor-store robbery had been arrested, and during questioning one of them confessed. The other two were still detained, however, pending tests to determine if either of them was the rapist. Logically, if the shoe print could be attributed to one particular man, then he was the murderer. But by now criminals and the lawyers who represent them are wise to the opportunities lying within the concept of reasonable doubt. A man could say his footprint was in a car because he had been given a lift in the vehicle, and even if that were highly unlikely it would constitute a reasonable doubt. The owner of the telltale shoes could also say he bought them second-hand – again, very convenient and hardly believable, but again it would have to be admitted as a factor creating reasonable doubt, especially in a serious criminal case.

'Where reasonable doubt finally falls down is when there are too many arrows pointing at the suspect,' said Hamill. 'When reasonable doubt turns into fantastically unreasonable doubt, then the system says whoa, hang on, we're not talking about coincidence or misapprehension here, this is plain guilt.'

In ideal circumstances, the DNA evidence from the semen specimens in two of the dead women, and from the nasal mucus found in the case of the third, should have been adequate to gain a conviction if a suspect's DNA proved to be a match. But there was a catch there, too, because defence attorneys are good at making juries believe that DNA profiling is desperately unreliable.

'We had to get the guilty party on multiple evidence,' said Lieutenant Marsh. 'None of the suspects' lawyers objected to us taking nasal swabs, which was ironic, because I know they would have kicked up six kinds of hell if we'd insisted on semen samples, yet the nasal DNA could be every bit as incriminating. So the tests were completed and if one came back as a match for the semen and mucus evidence from the three murders, we knew already who the guy was. But we like to kid ourselves we're civilised and we said nothing.'

In truth, Marsh had no doubt who the guilty party was and he admitted that he had difficulty stopping himself interrogating the man before the test results came back. 'We waited and waited, and finally back came the results. With a DNA analysis they always give you a probability figure, and in this case, the probability was that only six men in the entire United States could have deposited that DNA pattern inside the first two victims and on the tissue found beside Louise Kaplan's body, and one of those six was our prime suspect, Dudley Friar.

'When I saw the report I went at that guy like I was pulling a terrorist off my grandma. It's a glorious sensation, to be in an interrogation where you have no doubt at all. After all the years I've served in this job, that kind of feeling doesn't come too often, and I think I must have impressed the suspect with my shining certainty, because he folded in less than ten minutes and gave me all the details, including his belief that he raped and murdered women because when he was a kid he had been forced against his will to drink orange juice enriched with too many extra vitamins, especially vitamin E.'

Dudley Friar was twenty-nine. He worked at night as a hotel security guard and during the day did a clown act for children's parties, where he called himself Mr Sunshine. He had a record of petty theft and minor violence dating back to the age of fourteen; when he was twenty he had attempted to rape an undercover policewoman, and later succeeded in raping a female paramedic as she sat in a small park smoking a cigarette, only a short distance from a major accident scene she had just attended.

'I think a smart psychiatrist could have saved Dudley Friar a jail sentence,' Marsh said. 'He was definitely weird, and getting weirder.' But Friar did not want a psychiatrist speaking on his behalf because he believed there was a deep disgrace in any kind of mental illness and he wanted no one suggesting he was in any way insane. Besides, he was convinced that his problem was physical, an aggravation of certain normally dormant nerve centres by excessive fruit acid boosted with vitamin E.

'So we were free to prosecute a straight multiple rape and murder case, with no tricky psychological stuff coming in from the wings,' Marsh said. 'In the end we did a real hyperkill job with the evidence, but that's what was needed.'

A New York evening paper summarised the prosecution's parading of the proof.

Evidence was brought to show that fibres from cloth identical to that used in Friar's uniform were found at the scene of all three murders; the security company's badge worn on the front of Friar's cap fitted perfectly against a pattern of marks inside the third victim's car; a footprint found in the same car matched exactly the sole pattern from the right shoe of the pair Friar wore to work; the DNA profile of semen taken from victims one and two matched the DNA of mucus taken from a tissue found at the scene of the third murder – and the DNA in question was identical to that of Dudley Friar.

The jury convicted and Friar was sentenced to three terms of life imprisonment.

'A lot of guys quote that case as an example of DNA profiling catching a killer and putting him away,' Marsh said. 'But although I happen to believe in the accuracy of DNA profiling and its ability to pinpoint one human being out of millions, I also believe that if the DNA had been all we had, conclusive as it was, we would have lost that case.'

Dr Hamill agreed. 'Things are bound to change. The history of DNA profiling will harden into a catalogue of reliable identifications and it will be enough on its own to bring a conviction. But until then, the Dudley Friar case has to stand as the model for a solid conviction. It was a success for the prosecution because of investigative zeal, which is far too often lacking in present-day police work, if I may say so. I can't deny that the Friar case is often referred to as a success for the DNA scientists, but the fact is, good old-fashioned clue-chasing and plenty of uncomplicated evidence was what did the trick.'

Vengeance

'Until I was about twenty-nine, I didn't believe in such a thing as implacable badness,' said Dr Peter Kline, formerly a forensic pathologist with the Medical Examiner's Department of New York City. 'In spite of the job, my level of respect for humanity was pretty high. I was sure I had seen it all, but it was still clear to me there was unquenchable good in the worst, just as there was a measure of bad in the best, and that in the long, final analysis, mankind was profoundly decent.

'In short, I knew nothing. But as I say, until some time around my twenty-ninth birthday I hadn't encountered the truly black-hearted, the *wholly bad*. And then there it was, neatly packaged in one person who, my elders and betters promised me, was nothing like unique.'

At the time Dr Kline was speaking of, he was deputy head of a medical jurisprudence team set up to deal with the medico-legal aspects of serious assaults, 'domestic' homicides and other special cases. 'The Trask case was eight long years ago,' he said. 'It still looms back there as the one that shook the scales from my eyes.'

At 2.15 a.m. on Tuesday 18 November 1986, a night-duty police patrol was directed to an apartment block in the Melrose district of the Bronx, close to the Yankee Stadium. The elderly man who had phoned the police met them at the main door of the block and told them he had heard terrible screaming and the noise of breaking glass from the apartment opposite his own, where a couple named Trask lived. 'They're a quiet couple, respectable, they don't ever bother anybody. I just know something bad has happened . . .'

The police officers found the door of the Trasks' apartment partly open. The place was in darkness and there was no sound from inside. The senior of the two officers edged carefully along the narrow hall, shining his torch around him, noticing that picture frames were hanging at odd angles, a telephone table had been overturned and the telephone cable was ripped from the wall. 'It was warm in the apartment,' the officer noted in his report, 'and there was a distinct smell of blood.'

A woman moaned somewhere in the darkness beyond a bedroom door. One officer opened the door and the other found the light switch on the wall. When the light came on they both stared, unable for a moment to comprehend what they saw. Every piece of furniture in the room – the bed, the bedside cabinets, the dressing table, two tallboys and a linen chest – had been overturned. A large grey and pink rug was rucked up and rolled over at the centre, and at first sight the policemen assumed it was smeared with paint.

'There was just so much of it,' the senior officer said afterwards. 'It was swabbed across the carpet in stripes six inches wide in places, this dull red stuff, a really dense colour, and of course as we stood there we realised this was where the smell was coming from. It was blood, not paint. God knows how much of it was there. When we went right into the room we saw the man. He was lying behind the middle of the rolled-over carpet.'

The man was Michael Trask, thirty-eight, a self-employed electronic designer. He was naked and his body was stretched out full length, half turned from the waist. As the officers stepped closer they saw that his head had been cut off and was lying beside the body, upside down. The neck had been cut away close to the shoulders and the severed cartilage of the larynx lay flapped out on the hollow in the collarbone.

'We still hadn't seen the woman we'd heard moaning. My partner went across and looked under the bed, which was half upside down, leaning against the wall. The woman was under there, lying on the floor. She was completely naked. She was curled up tight like a baby and sobbing into her hands. Her face was all bloody.'

Between them the officers eased the woman out from under the bed and covered her with the quilt. The senior officer used his radio to call an ambulance, then he alerted the homicide division while his partner searched the rest of the apartment.

The ambulance and the homicide officers arrived at approximately the same time. They all began crowding into the apartment at once. The uniformed officers who had answered the call managed to direct the paramedics to the woman, who now seemed to be in shock. When she had been photographed in the context of the disrupted room, then close up so that the various marks on her face and arms would be faithfully recorded, she was taken to hospital. The detective in charge of the murder team, Lieutenant Charlie Grossett, assigned the two patrol officers to keep back neighbours and other spectators from the door, then set about overlaying order on the chaos in the apartment.

'Inevitably, things emerged piecemeal and out of order,' he recalled. 'Somebody discovered that a rear window was open and located a piece of dark fabric caught in the rotted outer woodwork of the window frame. Another guy established that the front door had been forced from the outside – his theory was that it had been done with one of those leverage devices they use for knocking down doors in illegal drug factories.

'The forensic collection team found a whole forest of things –
clumps of hair, splashes of blood in crazy inaccessible places,
slivers of broken fingernail . . . and then one of them working
in the dark alley at the back found a big cook's knife with a
twelve-inch blade. There was blood smeared all over the blade
and on the handle. It looked like it had been sharpened by an
expert – it was like a razor.'

This was not the worst murder case the Bronx had ever
seen, but because of the unusual nature of the killing –
deliberate decapitation requires a maniacal degree of intent
and is not seen very often – Dr Christopher Lawton was
asked to lend his expertise to the investigation at the scene.
Lawton was an expert at investigating crimes with overtly
psychotic elements. When he arrived he enlisted a former
protégé, Dr Peter Kline, who was already working at the
scene with his team, to take photographs. Kline was happy
to help Dr Lawton. 'I loved working with him,' he said. 'It
was a privilege, even though I knew I was being asked to
help because I'm good with a camera and I had all my own
equipment. That night, though, my fascination with Doc
Lawton's procedural work was not as intense as it could have
been. My attention was divided. I had seen mutilations
before – I saw them nearly every day – but that one, with the
guy's body so lithe and healthy-looking, so relaxed there on
the floor, almost like he was stretching after a sleep – but
with no goddamned head on . . . well, I don't know. It was
the visual paradox, I guess, and it didn't help that I was very
tired. Before I knew it I was feeling really ill.

'I struggled through the hour we were there, taking pictures
when Dr Lawton asked me, collecting specimens, making sure
the NYPD guys had identical specimens – I was just gofering
generally, but I didn't do any *hard* thinking about the case.
Even after I read the medical report on the woman, and after I
went back to the scene for a walk-through, I didn't entertain

any notion that the case was any way other than it appeared –
God knows, that was bad enough . . .'

The woman found lying under the overturned bed was
Angie Trask, thirty-four, the wife of the dead man. At the
hospital she was examined by two doctors working as a
diagnostic emergency team, while a third collected all the
samples necessary in a case of serious assault. The following
is an extract from a preliminary report by the doctors who
examined Angie Trask when she arrived at the accident and
emergency room.

Angela Mary Trask: Date of Birth 3/16/52

The patient is a well-nourished Caucasian female with
no superficial deformities. She has multiple bruising to the
legs, buttocks, arms and face, numerous abrasions and
small cuts on the arms, abdomen and face, and intermittent haemorrhage from both nostrils. The hair at her
crown is matted with blood and she has small wounds at
several points on her scalp. The knuckles of both hands
are swollen and three fingernails are broken. On arrival
the patient appeared to be in hypovolemic shock: her skin
was cold and pale, with blueness at the lips and fingers,
and she was confused and restless. Transfer to a supportive environment and the administration of a saline solution by drip raised temperature, improved skin tone and
restored correct mental orientation.

Bruising, scratching and localised swelling are evident
around the external genitals, and there is dried blood
around the anus. A speculum was used to examine the
vagina and a copious amount of a substance consistent
with the appearance and viscosity of semen has been
removed from around the neck of the cervix. The anterior
wall of the vagina is severely scratched.

The perimeter of the anus is cut in several places and

the opening appears patulous. Examination with a speculum shows that a hard rubber ball (identifiable as a squash ball) is lying in the cavity of the rectum: the high-friction surface of the ball appears to have caused considerable tissue damage to the anus and to the walls of the lower tract of the large bowel. It has been decided to leave the ball where it lies until it is safe to administer a general anaesthetic before it is removed.

Preliminary assessment of the patient, in the absence of firm corroboration, indicates she has been beaten and subjected to an unusual level of physical abuse that appears to have included rape. Following the initial evaluation her wounds have been cleaned, she has been given anti-tetanus medication and has now been passed to the care of a surgical team for specialised treatment.

'The police had total control of the crime scene for twelve hours,' Kline said, 'but in the end, when the dust began to settle, it fell to my little team to do a painstaking medico-legal work-up on the case. We were faced with a pile of evidence and an as yet unsubstantiated narrative of what happened in the Trasks' apartment that night. We started with what we knew, and set it all down in as close to a logical sequence as we could devise.'

The summary of circumstances attending the murder of Michael Trask and the rape and assault of his wife Angie ran as follows. Trask, an independent designer of compact and miniature electronic devices, had lived with his wife Angie, a community theatre set-designer and aspiring playwright, in the same second-floor apartment for three years. The apartment was in a fashionable sector of the Bronx, increasingly colonised by artists and independent business people since the mid-eighties.

In an interview tape-recorded from her hospital room Angie

told the police that on the evening of 17 November Michael had been working at home. He was in the process of designing a circuit for the remote opening of garage doors in an area of the city where conventional remote units had been found recently to interfere with the reception of satellite television. Michael had in fact completed the design and was at that time working on a compact casing for the unit. At some time around one in the morning, he decided to have a second and final drink of hot chocolate and then go to bed. Angie was still up, watching TV in the sitting room. They had a warm drink together and retired for the night.

Approximately an hour later Angie heard a noise at the apartment door. She woke Michael and they lay together listening. There was a sharp cracking sound, like wood breaking under pressure. Michael leaped out of bed and ran into the hall without pausing to put on a dressing gown.

Angie was scared and stayed where she was, but when she heard her husband cry out she grabbed the bedside telephone to call 911. The line was dead. Frightened as she was, she got out of bed and threw on a dressing gown. She dashed into the hall, brandishing a stout metal ruler from Michael's drawing kit, which lay open on a chair.

She had got only a little way along the hall when a man came at her with both hands extended, his feet thudding heavily on the carpet as he strode towards her. He picked her up bodily and threw her back into the bedroom. Angie said she hit her head on the lower edge of the dressing table and for a time she must have been stunned. When she came round, the overhead light in the bedroom was on and the man was kneeling on the rucked-up carpet. He was making broad sweeping movements with one hand as he held something down with the other.

'I lifted my head,' Angie said on the recording, 'and I was kind of looking along the length of my body and beyond me I could see this shape that the man was bending over. It dawned on me that the thing being held down was my husband, it was Michael, and the man was cutting him with a knife, a big knife, and it made a hissing and squelching sound as it cut through him. Michael wasn't resisting. I jumped up and I remember I felt sick and dizzy and faint all at the same time, but I got on my knees and I saw that Michael's neck was open like a horrible red mouth. Christ, it was unbelievable, I still can't believe it – the destruction of him, the change from what he was to that mess . . .'

The attacker turned when Angie got to her knees and she recognised him. He was Don Richards, a one-time friend of the couple. They had drifted apart as Richards' commercial success – he was in electronics, too – began to diminish at much the same rate as Michael's began to improve.

'He came at me, and I couldn't take my eyes off the knife,' she said. 'I remember I felt relieved for a second when he flung it away from him. But he kept coming at me and he was grinning in a horrible way, an angry way, and he grabbed me, picked me up the way he did out in the hall, and he hoisted me with a hand hooked between my legs and one grabbing my nightgown at my chest, and he slammed me against the wall. It knocked the air out of me. I started to pass out again.'

Seconds, or perhaps minutes, later, Angie did not know, she was conscious of being on the floor and Richards was wrecking the room, striding around overturning furniture, up-ending the bed, snarling 'Bastard!' and 'Two-timing shit!' and 'Thieving fucker!'

'And then he turned to me and knelt down and I knew what he was going to do. I tried to stop him but he was strong and rough and I truly thought he was going to kill me anyway, either before or after. He flattened me on the floor and came down on top of me. The pain was terrible, *terrible*, he used his fingers first, pulling me open like I was a drawstring bag. Then he groaned and grunted and pumped himself into me. When he had finished he rolled me on my face and there was this unbelievable pain as he shoved something into my backside – it felt like he was tearing me in two. I never felt pain like it.'

From then onwards, Angie said, consciousness came and went in overlapping phases. She remembered crawling towards the safety of the overturned bed, trying to creep away from her pain and the possibility of more hurt if she lay there exposed and vulnerable. The next thing she remembered clearly was being drawn out from under the bed by the two police officers.

'Our first job was to add Angie's statement to the evidence we had, and then to try to make a more detailed and coherent picture of the crime,' Kline said. 'A late addition to our evidence was that on the day Angie made her statement, police called at the apartment of Don Richards to question him, and found him dead with a gun in his hand. He had apparently shot himself through the head.'

Once the police and forensic technicians had left the Trasks' apartment, Kline and two of his associates did a 'walk-through' of the crime scene, a reconstruction based on testimony and evidence. Medical teams are often assigned this task when the bulk of the evidence falls into the medico-legal category.

'Starting at the front door, we ploughed our way through the scenario as Angie had drawn it, making changes where she must have been mistaken, or where she had left a gap and we could fill it because of some residual clue.'

It appeared that events had occurred more or less as Angie Trask had described them to the police. For whatever reason, Don Richards had come to the apartment with murderous intent and he had carried out his plan briskly with no hesitation or doubt. The only wonder to Kline was that Richards hadn't killed Angie too.

By this time Angie had been encouraged by a counselling psychiatrist to think carefully about the attack on herself. She had done that, and she now believed that Richards had performed on her body something which, for him, was the ultimate and most extreme thing he could do, the thing she had known all along he wanted to do, and had been forbidden by her to try.

'He made a move on me way back. I told him in very clear terms that I was not available. He accepted the position, on the surface anyway, but I know he went on wanting me – he was the obsessive type and it was easy to tell how he felt. But at the same time he was scared of ever trying, because he wasn't the kind who could handle rejection – I could see that when I warned him off the first time.'

Also, she believed, Richards would not have been able to withstand the consequences if Michael Trask had found out about his advances. Richards was a man who could not countenance showdowns – he had admitted that to both Angie and Michael, and they had seen evidence of it when he accidentally came into conflict with people in business, or even during minor disagreements at parties.

'So the more I think about that, and about the way he was that night he broke in – he was, you know, *avid* – the more I think, yeah, he snapped, he turned right round and he did the ultimate to me, he did what he came to do, and the thing with the ball, that was my punishment for rejecting him in the first place, right?'

While Kline and his associates were putting together their report on the crime scene, he heard that Dr Lawton was having trouble with his evaluation of the case. 'For my own part, I was having no problems with the case at all,' Kline said. 'There was no prosecution going ahead, and no manhunt of any kind; there was no rush, the case would be put straight on file when we were through. So we were putting together the documentation with a certain amount of leisure, and for once my thoughts had time to gel and to be recognised for what they were. I had

Death of A Call Girl: Vanessa Clyde, photographed by Joseph Campbell a few weeks before he killed her.

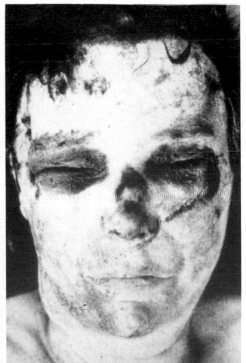

Vanessa Clyde, photographed shortly after her body was found hanging on a fence.

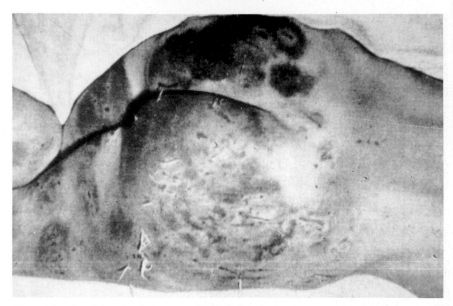

Extensive bruising on Vanessa Clyde's lower body, produced by savage kicking.

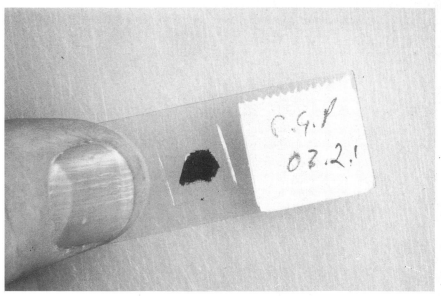

The larger of the fragments taken from under Vanessa Clyde's fingernails.

Burning: Clear impression of a knife handle found in sandy earth near the burned-out car.

Per Moberg's knife, after the police had cleaned it.

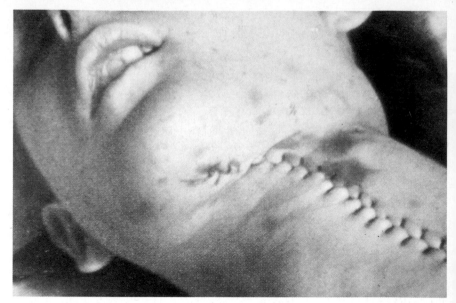

Hyperkill: The marks of strangulation on Louise Kaplan's neck (stitches were inserted following the autopsy).

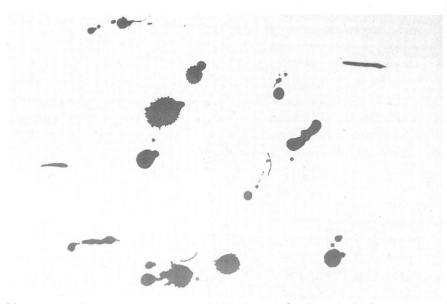

Vengeance: Average appearance of blood spots from a relatively static source.

no misgivings, no suspicions that things were not as they appeared. I don't think my views would have turned out any different if I had been under pressure, but I know now that under pressure I am apt to function a lot better.'

If it had not been for Dr Lawton's doubts, Kline added, the investigation might not have changed direction when it did. 'I think the police would have gone quite a distance down the road to wrapping the whole thing up and filing it on a shelf before anybody smelled a rat.'

Dr Lawton had been completing his own written observations on the Trask case, illustrated with a number of Kline's photographs, when he noticed something that set off a whole train of doubts. He drew Kline's attention to the photographs. In particular, Lawton was interested in close-ups of drops of blood in the bedroom. These had been sampled and were known to be Michael Trask's blood. The drops occurred in groups and they all had one thing in common.

'They are what they look like,' Lawton told Kline. 'They are drops. They are not splashes. This man was hacked to death, he had his head cut off. You are a pathologist, you know that when a subject is cut, even when you work at moderate speed, oblique splashes will inevitably occur as you cut off major parts.'

Kline felt a fool for missing the discrepancy. 'Blood drops and splashes are important, very important,' he said. 'They're indicators of past events at a crime scene. When a quantity of free blood flies through the air, the shape of the resulting splash can show the direction of travel, and therefore the location and position of the weapon – and splashes can often indicate the minimum number of blows that were struck. A blood drop moving through the air is preceded by a small globule, and when it hits a surface at an angle to its direction of travel, it produces a splash that looks a lot like an exclamation mark, with the dot at the leading end. These blood deposits didn't look like that.'

No blood splashes had been found on the walls, either, except for a few which looked more like daubs and dabs than splashes. The pictures clearly showed circular drops of blood, indicating a static source. 'When blood drops straight down on to the floor from a non-moving point, it will always make near-perfect circles – sometimes jagged edged, like starburst shapes, but neat circles all the same.'

It was Lawton's opinion that Michael Trask had not been hacked to death as his wife said. To produce such undramatic blood traces, the decapitation must have been performed methodically, the head being cut from the body rather slowly.

Another discrepancy troubling Lawton was the time of death estimation in the autopsy report on Don Richards. This is a very difficult part of the forensic pathologist's job, an area where it is never possible to be precise, and a particular time is never indicated. Instead, a 'bracket' is given, stating the longest and shortest likely times since death occurred. In the case of Richards, extra-special care had been taken, because the man in charge of the autopsy had a reputation as an authority on the various ways of estimating times of death.

'The pathologist had used three separate methods to arrive at an estimate,' Kline said, 'and what he found was that Richards had died somewhere between midnight on 16 November and noon on the 17th. No earlier, no later. In view of the implications, Dr Lawton took the unusual step of examining the notes and lab findings on the three estimations, and he had to agree with the findings.'

So Don Richards had died more than twelve hours – at least – before Michael Trask was murdered.

Kline said he began to feel like an idiot. 'It's so easy to miss something vital, something that can turn a case right round. Now, of course, I did feel I had been missing something – in fact a number of things – and to make the feeling worse, there was the distinct possibility that I'd had this done to me deliberately. I'd been dealt a whole hand off the bottom of the deck. Every forensic worker – pathologist, lawyer, chemist, shrink, whatever – is spooked at the thought of being deliberately and successfully fooled.'

All concerns about discrepancies in the case were set aside for the moment: Angie Trask had clearly been lying, and since she was the only person left alive in a case involving only three people, all suspicion had to focus on her. Accordingly, her statement was dissected and every major point was checked. The story began to fall apart.

'For example,' Kline said, 'the clumps of Angie's hair we found on the floor of the bedroom: when they were examined it was found that they had been cut off, not yanked out as she had told us. The appearance wasn't bad – it matched the story, because she had cut close to the scalp – but once the lie was exposed, when you looked at those sharp cut ends under a magnifier, the whole case began to look like a flimsy amateur scam just waiting to be pulled apart.'

Detectives were assigned to check Angie Trask's background. They were encouraged to follow all leads. Meanwhile, Kline made some discoveries on his own. 'It was the small wounds, mainly the scratches on her face, arms and legs,' he said. 'They were pretty obviously self-inflicted – "obviously" now that I was primed to be suspicious, of course. The thing about scratches in an assault is that they're random, they're all over the place. You can safely say their distribution from side to side of the victim will be about even. Self-inflicted scratches, on the other hand, tend to be a little one-sided – or, as in Angie's case, a lot one-sided – always on the side away from the leading hand. In other words, right-handed people injure their left side more, and vice versa. Also the marks have a certain regularity in their appearance, and they avoid really sensitive areas like the eyes. Once I had noticed these latest discrepancies, I promised myself that from there on in, I wouldn't believe even the most innocent-looking feature of the case until I had concrete proof.'

There was a development in the matter of the squash ball that had been inserted in Angie's anus. The surgeon who removed the ball noted on his report that 'the anus has slightly keratinised edges, and on close inspection appeared to be chronically abraded'. This meant that Angie was not entirely unaccustomed to having objects pushed into her anus, and indeed the keratinised edges (keratin is the fibrous protein found in hard skin) and the chronic abrasion are typical of people who habitually indulge in passive anal intercourse.

The surgeon further expressed his opinion that the cuts around the anus and the scratch injuries inside had not been incidentally induced by the presence of the ball, because the abrasions did not correspond to the kind of marks the ball would make. A gynaecologist was asked to submit an opinion. He said that the multiple small wounds resembled nothing so much as fingernail scratches – 'a woman's fingernails,' he added, drawing attention to the fact that the cuts were short and steeply arced, like the tips of carefully filed small fingernails.

Shortly afterwards, the ballistics laboratory reported that while the gun found in the hand of Don Richards was certainly the one that shot him, there was no conceivable way he could have fired it himself.

'The angle was wrong,' Kline said. 'He would have had to have held his hand in an extremely painful position, from which squeezing the trigger would have been all but impossible. Even if he had done that, there was no way the gun could have ended up lying naturally between his fingers the way it was when the police found his body. The feeling was that this was just a replay of an old ploy: the gun had been used by someone else who then put it in the dead man's fingers, believing that would fool the police.'

The autopsy on Richards had included the removal of blood samples and stomach contents for laboratory examination. When the analysis of stomach contents came back it indicated the presence of a high concentration of the commercial sedative drug Amytal. Blood samples also showed the presence of the drug in a correspondingly high amount.

'In an age of subtlety in the execution of a premeditated crime, this was beginning to look silly,' Kline said. 'We were pretty sure by now that Angie had killed both men. Instead of confronting her with what we now had, however, the police felt it might be a good idea to find more evidence before she had the chance to put a lawyer on the case. The way the evidence was coming, we felt we could stack it up until we had enough to burn her eight times over. That might seem like excessive punitive zeal, but when you consider the way lawyers can create the illusion of reasonable doubt in a court these days, an evidential glut would be no bad thing.'

Lieutenant Charlie Grossett interviewed a restaurant owner in the borough of Queens who knew Don Richards so well that he regarded him as one of his special customers. 'This guy said that Richards was a real happy fellow, his business was doing well and he was quite the big spender,' Lieutenant Grossett explained. 'He also said he was a ladies' man, always coming into the place with different women, showing them a good time.' Grossett produced a sheaf of photographs from the proprietor's collection showing various different people eating at the restaurant. Two pictures showed Don Richards and Angie at a table together, smiling for the camera. They had been taken ten days before Richards died.

'The feeling among the restaurant staff,' Grossett continued, 'was that these two were going to be an item some day, because although Richards still brought in other women, on that last occasion Angie Trask appeared very emotional and it looked like they were getting really serious about each other.'

Kline and the others on his team, accustomed to reasonably challenging criminal scenarios, could hardly believe what was happening in this case. It was as if Angie Trask had set herself up to be condemned for capital murder. Shortly after Grossett came up with the photographs, another detective obtained a bill of sale for the 9mm Heckler and Koch pistol with which Don Richards had been killed. It had been sold to Angie Trask, who had not even troubled to falsify her name.

The flow of evidence accelerated. A salesman in a Fifth Avenue department store recalled selling the knife used to decapitate Michael Trask; it was a very expensive instrument and was even stamped with a unique serial number. It had been sold to an account-card holder, and when the number was checked it was found to be the account of Angie Trask.

A laboratory analysis of the swab taken from Angie's cervix showed that the semen did not belong to Don Richards. A specimen removed from the body of Michael Trask produced an exact match.

Kline, at the prompting of Dr Lawton, re-examined the mutilations on Michael Trask and confirmed that the apparently haphazard cutting around the neck was a series of quite deliberate pressure cuts rather than slashes. The condition of the cut edges of skin and tissue showed that, at the beginning of the decapitation, Trask had been alive, which raised the question of how he had been subdued. An analysis of his blood was ordered. When the results came back, they showed a very high concentration of the powerful sedative drug amobarbital.

Two detectives working the drugstores and all-night pharmacies came up with a prescription for Amytal, a commercial brand of amobarbital, in the name of Angie Trask. The doctor who issued the prescription was located and was able to confirm that he had prescribed amobarbital to this patient a number of times as a sleeping drug.

'The police decided that with what they were now sitting on, it was time they pulled Angie in,' said Kline.

What they had, Lieutenant Grossett believed, was a woman whose approach to setting up a crime was exactly the same, in its concept, as setting up a stage show: 'And she was a set-designer, right? In the theatre appearances are everything, the underpinning hardly matters so long as the effect is good and the illusion holds. But this woman took no account of the fact that in crime investigation the appearances are pushed aside so that the facts show and can be examined. It was as if that was something beyond her comprehension, something she couldn't even conceive of.'

On the strength of the accumulated evidence, Angie Trask was charged with the murders of her husband and Don Richards. After a few minutes of protesting her innocence she stopped suddenly and shrugged. 'Well, all right, yes,' she said, almost impatiently, 'I did it, I killed them, both of them.' She added that if she had the opportunity, she would do it again – only next time she would make sure they suffered more. 'For me, neither one of them could have hurt enough.'

Her husband, she said, had been seeing another woman, the secretary of one of his clients. This in itself had not been enough to make Angie angry, since she had been having an affair with Don Richards for more than a year. The trouble was that her husband had been planning to leave her, get a divorce and marry the other woman. He had actually confided as much to Don Richards.

'Don told me about it,' Angie said, 'and at the same time that he told me, I could see he was getting ready to drop me. It was one thing to have me around for decoration and for a good screw when he wanted it, but as a liability he did not want me at all. He didn't have to tell me that. Some things are said loudest by a look in the eyes.

'To top it all, I found out that my husband had been bleeding our savings and our joint capital into another account someplace else. Not only was I going to be ditched, but I was going to be left without much money, and I wouldn't have Don to rely on. Fat chance. So, from having a reasonable life with a touch of excitement in the background, I was headed for a ghastly and permanent drabsville.'

As time passed and she watched the small signs of her husband preparing to leave her for good, Angie found that Don Richards did not want to see her so much. Once, a little more than a week before he died, he took her out for dinner, but it was in the nature of a farewell, a gentle unloading of Angie into the arms of a fate that would not involve Don in any way. 'I was going to kill myself,' she said, 'I was going to use the Amytal. Then I thought, why the fuck should I do that? I didn't hate me, I hated *them*. I gave it some thought, and the idea of killing them just kind of dawned on me, warm, like sunlight.'

She became very serious on the point. She told Lieutenant Grossett that the thought of killing someone is a thought that everybody gets from time to time, but the thought of doing it as a serious, feasible exercise is something entirely different; it has an allure. 'I planned it for a week, then I went ahead and did it. I went to see Don on a pretext – to ask for a reference for a job: I told him I'd decided to try for a fresh start in LA – and I took the Amytal with me. It was the powder out of ten capsules, and I put it in his coffee, which he liked strong. I made it extra strong while he wrote out my reference. He conked out maybe ten minutes after taking the coffee. I washed the cup, waited till I was sure he was well down into sleep, then I did the bit with the gun. I have to say it was one of the easiest things I ever did.'

The only startling part, she said, was the noise. Don's visible transition from pink-faced life to waxy death was nothing dramatic. He even bled a lot less than she had expected.

'Back at the apartment that night I did the same to Michael, except first I got him to fuck me, which wasn't entirely easy, but I needed semen in me to keep the plot consistent. I spread the Amytal between a couple of mugs of hot chocolate which were his nightly ritual. He keeled over getting his socks off. I went around messing up the place, overturning everything and pulling up the bedroom rug. I put force marks on the door with a claw hammer and hung a rag I took from Don's place on the windowsill.

'Then I worked on myself, scratching myself up, beating myself on the head with a steak tenderiser, and all the other stuff. I can take certain kinds of pain, it's not a problem – in fact in some directions it's just the opposite. The ball would look like a real sadistic touch, I thought – even though it was a masochistic diversion, I know that now, it was just a sudden whim I had. Anyway, when I'd made myself into a victim, I pulled Michael into the middle of the floor and started on him with the knife.'

Again, she said, she felt no particular reaction to the fact that a human being was being killed Nor was there any revulsion at the messiness of the decapitation. 'Maybe it was the powerful symbolism that made me feel more kind of *vindicated* than anything else. I believed he needed what I was doing to him. I hated him, remember.' She paused. 'I still hate him. I hate all three of them.'

'All three?' Grossett said.

'Yes.'

'You mean the woman your husband was seeing? Her too?'

'That's right,' Angie said coolly. 'Her name is Maisie Haxton.' She hesitated and smiled faintly. 'I toyed with not telling you this, but thinking about it, what the hell – I invited her round for a talk two days before I killed Michael. She's in our garage.'

Twenty minutes later the police opened the up-and-over door of garage number 8 at the Trasks' apartment block. Inside they found a workbench, a tidy rack of car tools, and a plastic sack. Inside the sack was the body of a young woman. She wore a smart business suit which was bizarrely at odds with the rest of her appearance. Her eyes had been pierced with corn-cob skewers and her mouth was packed with cotton wool (Angie had drugged her and suffocated her by poking the wool down her throat with a knitting needle).

Angie explained how she had taken the body down in the service elevator on a bale truck and planned to move it from the garage to the garbage incinerator as soon as the deaths of Michael and Don had blown over.

'I had to tell her,' Kline said, 'that I could not understand how anybody could have such an elaborate murder scheme, carry it out as planned, and yet do so little background work – so little, in fact, that she was bound to get caught.'

Angie replied that she had concentrated principally on killing three people, and the only serious precautions she took were those which would ensure her plans would not be interrupted. 'And like I said, I would do it again. I would recommend it to other women.'

Dr Lawton believed that if Angie's hatred had not been such a powerfully distorting influence on her judgement, she might have taken more care. She was distracted by the heat of vengeance, he said, instead of acting in cold hatred.

'The theory part was irrelevant to me after I'd talked to her,' Kline said. 'It was obvious to me, staring into her face, that this woman was capable of anything. She said she would kill again if she had to, and she meant it. Worse than that, you could tell she would go out of her way to kill someone. Nobody in the world would be safe from a person like that once she had turned against them.'

Angie Trask was tried and found guilty on three counts of first-degree murder. She was sentenced to imprisonment for life in a state correction facility.

Bird Man

'Everything Eddie ever did, he did for show,' said Detective Inspector Ivan Pace. 'Even the business with the birds, when he bought all different kinds from breeders up and down the country and put them in cages and a big aviary in his back garden – he started all that on an urge to show off, after the publicity the Burt Lancaster film got. Eddie wanted to be thought of as somebody a bit outstanding, a special kind of man.'

Eddie Lawrence saw the film *Birdman of Alcatraz* in 1962 when he was twenty-eight. He was a fully appreticed and qualified carpenter and at that time he was working with a council maintenance crew in south-west London. By the age of twenty-six he had served two short jail sentences for being an accessory to burglary. Rather more exotically, he had spread the rumour, through gullible pals and girlfriends, that he was the mastermind behind a long unsolved series of safety-deposit burglaries in the West End and at the premises of two banks in the City.

'Twice we had him in for questioning, more to try to scare him into behaving himself than for any other reason,' said DI Pace. 'Out in public he always implied he knew a lot about big-time crime: he said he had been involved in it, as a specialist, for years; he claimed he had learned about explosives during his national service and that he had done some undercover safe-blowing in East Germany on behalf of the government. When he talked to us he was different. He never admitted that he bragged about being a big-time safe man, but he admitted he liked to exaggerate. "I'm harmless," he'd tell us, and we'd tell him we knew that, but he should stop pretending he wasn't.'

At that time the police believed petty theft was the worst crime Eddie Lawrence was ever likely to commit. When it was alleged that he was capable of doing grievous harm to another human being, and that he had in fact killed someone, none of the police officers who knew him would believe it. 'Eddie was a bit of a character, that was all,' Pace said. 'There were no hints of anything sombre or unpleasantly covert about his nature. When we first got the whisper that he was a murderer, he was in the early stages of his bird man incarnation – every other day new stories were circulating about Eddie spending his windfall on birds and special wire to shut in areas of his garden to make an aviary like the Snowdon enclosure at London Zoo.'

The windfall was £850, which had been left to him in the will of Cynthia Hambleton, a retired schoolteacher for whom he did odd jobs over a period of years and whose garden he had regularly tended. Cynthia had taught Eddie at secondary school, and it was generally felt he had a lingering affection for her, because he had never taken a penny for all the work he had done at her house and in her garden.

'The whisper, specifically, was that Eddie had murdered a woman in Stepney two years earlier, when he had been on contract loan to Stepney Council doing window reframing on a couple of their housing estates. The accusation was anonymous and very vague, and we were not inclined to believe any of it. But the informant persisted, and we began getting letters and even telegrams telling us we had to take the accusation seriously. In the end, after three months of this steady barrage, we felt obliged to look into the allegation.'

Eddie's history for a four-year period was researched and sifted for any hints of a hidden side to his nature. Nothing emerged until six days from the cut-off time Pace had stipulated for the investigation. A pub landlord in Stepney told a detective how he believed the joiner in question, 'Cocky Eddie' as he had been nicknamed in the bar, had mistaken him for a pimp. 'I don't know where he got hold of the idea – maybe somebody was winding him up – but he wouldn't believe he'd got the wrong man,' the landlord said. 'He kept on at me, any chance he got, whenever he'd had a few pints and was a bit glazed. He said he was after a blonde who was a bit unconventional, and it didn't matter if she wasn't a real blonde, as long as she looked blonde.'

Two of Eddie's former workmates in Stepney were interviewed a second time. At the first interview both men had said he was just a likeable loudmouth, a man with an odd assortment of vanities and foibles who was, nevertheless, all on the surface. But now, when the matter of his sexual tastes was raised, one of the men said that once or twice Eddie had shown an interest in local prostitutes.

'He came back from buying sandwiches one time,' the man said, 'and on the way he'd stopped in at three or four phone boxes and copied down the details and numbers the prostitutes left on the walls. He asked me if I thought it would cost much if he visited one of them. I told him I'd no idea, and he said it was something he would like to try just once, to know what it was like.' The interviewee had never discovered whether Eddie had called any of the numbers he collected, because soon afterwards they were put to work on separate squads.

'The woman he was alleged to have killed had in fact been a part-time prostitute,' DI Pace said. 'She was an artificial blonde, too – hardly a clinching collision of facts, but that aside, there was enough now to justify more serious digging.'

The dead woman, Laura Bingley, had been found in a derelict cellar three streets from the one-room flat where she lived and where she usually took her customers. The post-mortem record showed that she had apparently died of natural causes. A note added by the forensic pathologist explained:

Although the deceased was young she could not be assumed to have the normal resilience of youth. She was badly undernourished and had an emaciated appearance such as one sees in cases of slow starvation. The records of sudden death contain many cases similar to this, where the abrupt arrest of the heart appears to have been the primary cause of death, occasioned by a low constitutional resistance to cold and any sudden drop in the blood's balance of electrolytes.

'The only odd feature of the death was that Laura was found at a place no one had ever known her go before,' Pace said. 'The pathologist had confirmed that she'd had sexual intercourse close to the time she died, so someone had seen her either shortly before she died, or when she actually did die, but until now no suspicion attached to the person and no attempt had ever been made to trace him.'

Now a serious attempt was made. Two years had passed and memories had dimmed, but one person did have reason to remember Laura Bingley's movements on the night she died. Captain Eva Bristow of the Salvation Army had kept a motherly eye on a number of the prostitutes in the area, and she had several times talked to Laura, who had always seemed too frail for the kind of life she led.

'The poor dear was built like a sparrow,' Captain Bristow said. 'When we used to go into the pub to sing a hymn and sell our paper I would often see her with half a pint of stout, which somebody had told her was as good as a meal. The poor soul believed it. She always had a cigarette going, too, because she believed nicotine kept down infections. Laura was a sorry soul, a born victim from the look of her, and that last night I saw her I thought a couple of times, watching her, that she wasn't going to last much longer.'

Captain Bristow remember that Laura had been approached by several men, and finally got up and left with one of them. 'I've never forgotten him, for a number of reasons. Mainly he stuck in my mind because I thought, how can you do it, how can a grown man with a God-given moral conscience take out his baser lusts on a creature so frail and so sick-looking? Also, he bought a paper from me a few minutes before I saw him approach Laura, and I smelled lily-of-the-valley off him – my mother's favourite flower and a beloved scent from childhood. Oh yes, I remember him, all right.'

She described Eddie Lawrence perfectly, right down to the troublesome strands of hair that kept falling over his forehead and which he was constantly pushing back. A policewoman confirmed the part about the lily-of-the-valley: 'It's a real cheap, stinky cologne he uses, I've noticed it every time he's been in here. Sometimes the smell of his sweat masks it, mind you.'

So Eddie Lawrence was being accused, anonymously, of killing a woman he had almost certainly been with at or near the time she died. Extensive inquiries had failed to produce a witness who had seen Laura alive after she left the pub that night, but Pace did not feel he needed corroboration of Captain Bristow's story. 'What I really wanted to know was who was accusing Eddie, and on that score we got a result shortly after we spoke to Captain Bristow.'

A qualified document-examiner had determined that the carefully hand-printed anonymous letters had all been written on the same paper, and that the paper was from a rather expensive pad produced by a manufacturer of high-quality stationery to the legal profession. The ink, furthermore, was from the same company. Detectives visited the distribution department of the stationer's and were encouraged when they learned that the paper was not sold to many people in the UK – such expensive materials usually found a stronger market abroad. The detectives were given the names of twenty-seven companies in and around London which used the pads in question.

'It could have been a hard slog,' Pace said, 'checking the employee lists at all twenty-seven places, then rummaging in their backgrounds to find out who might have a reason to take a vengeful interest in the death of a prostitute two years before. But we got very lucky. At the fourth place, a firm of solicitors in Hackney, just a couple of miles north of the place where Laura Bingley died, the office manager we spoke to said it was funny we were asking about that particular paper, because somebody had stolen a brand-new pad of it off a desk in the senior partner's office, and they had all suspected the cleaner, who had left a few weeks later. So one of my officers asked if they'd happened to lose any ink too, and the man said, "Well, yes we did, as a matter of fact, a whole big bottle of it. How did you know that?" '

The police followed up the theory that the cleaner had stolen the paper and ink. They obtained her name and address from the files and the same afternoon two detectives called at a modest terraced house in Stepney and spoke to the sole occupant, a middle-aged widow called Esther Grant. The police asked if they could come in, and almost the first thing they saw was the pad of legal paper lying on the living-room table. On the sideboard was the tall bottle of blue-black ink with a couple of old-fashioned school dip-and-write pens lying alongside it.

'Esther Grant folded without any pressure,' Pace said. 'She told the officers that before her husband died the pair of them used to drink in the pub where Laura and a couple of other girls sat around waiting for trade. Like Captain Bristow, Esther was sorry for Laura, in fact she was pretty sorry for all the girls on the game around those parts.'

Esther had begun going to the pub alone at the time her husband entered hospital with a terminal cancer. She had done it as an exercise in self-sufficiency, she explained, because she knew the time was coming when she would have to do things on her own. On her third or fourth solo outing, she began talking to a few of the prostitutes, and she found their company agreeable. Then had come the terrible time when Esther's husband died, and in the aftermath she worked hard at living life alone. She continued to visit the pub on her own, and by now she knew most of the prostitutes by name.

'They kept themselves on one side, making no trouble for the rest of the public,' Esther told the police. 'The landlord's a live-and-let-live sort of chap and he didn't mind them being there as long as it didn't hurt his trade. He began to make jokes, gentle ones mind you, about me joining up with the girls, and I told him straight, that now I was on my own, they were a lifeline for me. They were a really friendly lot.'

At the time Laura Bingley died there had been great sadness among the other girls, Esther said. Then one night she spoke to one of them who appeared very agitated. Finally the prostitute said she would tell Esther what was wrong, as long as she didn't breathe a word to anybody else. 'I was the standard confessor to most of them by that time,' Esther said. 'They could tell me what they liked, it seemed to help them to do that, and of course, whatever they said, it stopped with me, it never went any further. And this girl, she told me she'd been with this really weird man who had told her he'd killed Laura. He'd killed her as an experiment in a way he'd learned from experts, so she'd better watch out.'

Esther had tried to reassure the girl by telling her it was just nonsense – Laura had died of natural causes, a post-mortem had shown that. But the girl was convinced the man had been telling the truth. She knew when they were telling the truth, she said, you learned how to detect a lie a mile off in her line of business. She also believed that if she did anything to cause the man any annoyance, she would suffer for it – probably the way Laura had suffered.

'And I didn't need to be told who the man was – I wouldn't have asked anyway – because whenever he came into the place, which he did quite a lot in those days, this girl would look as if she had been pole-axed. She literally stiffened and got herself out of sight so that he wouldn't approach her.'

Esther had learned the man's name – Eddie Lawrence – and she had started watching him. When she noticed that he left the pub a couple of times with one particular girl, Amy, she managed to get the girl to talk about him, broaching the subject by a roundabout route, saying he looked like a jolly and friendly type, which he did. Amy said that it was all a front. He was a weirdo, and if it weren't for the fact that he paid over the odds, she wouldn't have anything to do with him.

'She said she had a quick run through his jacket pocket when he was in the lavatory at her flat,' Esther said, 'and she found a big needle, like a surgical needle, with what looked like another needle up the centre of it. It was wrapped in a handkerchief, she said, and to her it looked terribly ominous.'

Why, a detective asked Esther, had she begun the campaign of accusation against Eddie Lawrence? And why wait so long?

'Because he bragged about little Laura again, about how he killed her,' Esther said. 'It was about four months ago. He showed up in Stepney again, and he picked up one of the girls in the pub and she was upset when she got back. I talked to her, and she told me he had been really weird. He took some kind of tablets, a couple she thought, on the way over to her flat, and after they had done their business he asked her if she remembered Laura.'

The girl had said she never knew Laura but she knew about her, and Eddie allegedly said he had known her, all right – he was the one who had killed her. And as he said it he tapped his breast pocket, the pocket where Amy had said he kept the strange needle.

'I don't know how I got to be so convinced that it was true he'd killed Laura,' Esther said, 'but I *was* convinced and I still am. Maybe it was the girls being so sure – they may be silly-headed things in a lot of ways, but when it comes to judging men, they're a lot brighter than the average person.'

Eddie had told Amy that he was from Fulham. A check of the electoral register confirmed that, and Esther then knew which police station to bombard with her anonymous messages.

It was ironic that Esther had stolen the legal pad and the ink in order to secure the anonymity of her letters. 'I didn't know the paper was expensive, or very special for that matter,' she said. 'I just wanted something that couldn't be placed as coming from a shop around these parts. It helped me to feel invisible too, if you understand what I mean.'

A doctor told DI Pace that the needle Amy had described sounded very much like a spinal needle, which has a comparatively wide bore, is quite long and has a stylette along its centre which keeps the needle clear and provides minimal suction when it is removed just before spinal fluid is drawn off.

'A whole reappraisal of Eddie Lawrence was called for,' Pace said. 'That's what I decided, and fortunately my boss was similarly inclined, so before long we were digging deep, with plenty of manpower to handle the job. The first interesting nugget to surface was that during Eddie's second term in prison, he had been befriended by a pharmacist doing ten years for drug-trafficking offences. He had got Eddie interested in the 'mind-settling' properties of a drug called Daprisal. A follow-up on the outside with some one-time soft-drug dealers had confirmed that Eddie had been put in touch with an illegal source of the prescription drug. 'Eddie also got the pharmacist to tell him some scary medical stuff, and one of the topics they got on to was untraceable methods of murder.'

The pharmacist, still a prisoner at the time of the investigation into Eddie Lawrence's background, was keen to do anything that would show him in a civically responsible light. Accordingly, he told the police everything he and Eddie had talked about, although a detective guessed that he did so also because he thought that Eddie was on the outside doing the same kind of demolition job on him.

Indeed, yes, the pharmacist said, the use of a spinal needle had been discussed; Eddie had even asked him to write down the name of the item. Specifically, the pharmacist had explained to Eddie how it was possible to kill someone with a spinal needle by draining off an excessive amount of spinal fluid. Eddie had pressed the pharmacist to give him explicit details, and had even asked for sketches to be made. The particular part of the operation he wanted to be sure about was how to angle the tip of the needle thirty degrees towards the subject's head when inserting it between the bones of the spine in order to reach the spinal cord.

'The pharmacist said he kept on at him about that,' Pace said, 'about how you had to imagine a certain plane when the needle went in, and then work at angles from an imagined straight line. The skilled carpenter in Eddie could appreciate a need for precision, but the obsession with precision in the service of killing was an aspect of Eddie's character I would never have suspected.'

The wholesale digging into Eddie's past produced a picture

of a man superficially vain and harmless, but covertly obses-
sional. A search of records at the local public library showed
that during a one-year period he had borrowed books on
tropical bird management, sexual deviation and surgical procedures for nurses.

'A logical next step might have been to exhume the body of
Laura Bingley,' Pace said. 'On the face of it, there was a case
for doing that, but it was academic since Laura had been
cremated. Strictly speaking, we couldn't do anything about
Eddie, because in the absence of a body and any hard evidence
linking him to the death of Laura Bingley, the police had no
right to set foot in his living space. But then, while we were in
the middle of making a decision about whether or not we
should confront him with what we knew, we got lucky a second
time.'

Discreet inquiries at a factory where Eddie had been working part-time as a cabinet finisher produced the testimony of an
elderly night security guard, Terry Latham. Terry said that
some evenings, Eddie would drop into the yard on his way
home from the pub, and he would sit with him to keep him
company. Terry did not particularly want anybody keeping
him company, since he liked being on his own, and he found
Eddie's patter rather too lightweight to be of interest. However, on a couple of occasions, Eddie had talked about his old
schoolteacher, Cynthia Hambleton, for whom he had done
odd jobs and looked after the garden.

'He told me how much he'd secretly hated her,' Terry
Latham told the police. 'For a couple of years at school she had
made his life hell, he said – embarrassing him in front of the
others when he couldn't read without stammering and stum-
bling, making him stay late to write lines, all that nonsense.
When he heard she'd retired to a house round the corner from
where he lived, he moved in on her. He said he used to piss all
over her flowers, vandalise her pot plants and blame it on cats,

poison the goldfish in her pond, and all while he looked like he was tending to the upkeep of the place.'

The most sinister part, though, Terry said, had been when Eddie told him he had bumped off Cynthia Hambleton when she had taken to her bed with bronchitis. She had already told him there was something for him in her will, so he decided to bring forward the day when he would receive it. 'I didn't believe him at first, and he never mentioned it again,' Terry said. 'But when I'd thought about it, it occurred to me he was serious when he told me that. It wasn't told to me like some of the rubbish he talked. It was true, I fancied.'

When Terry was asked why he hadn't come forward with what he believed to be possible evidence of a murder, he said he was not one to seek out the law, for whatever reason. 'When they come to me, though, I can be quite forthcoming . . .'

Cynthia Hambleton had not been cremated. An exhumation order was obtained for her body and a forensic pathologist performed an autopsy on the decomposed remains under the supervision of a consultant neurosurgeon and a neuropathologist. 'It was clear, even in a body so badly broken down by putrefaction, that the brain and spinal cord had been severely deprived of fluid, which would inevitably have led to death,' was the pathologist's finding. He went on to describe marks on the tissue covering the lumbar vertebrae, and punctures in the membranes at the third and fourth lumbar interspaces consistent with the invasion of a spinal needle.

'On the verbal evidence of Terry Latham, and on the evidence of the post-mortem findings, Eddie Lawrence was charged with murder,' Pace said. 'At the trial the neurosurgeon said it would have been easy for anyone keen enough to learn to do what Eddie had done to Cynthia Hambleton without her feeling much in the way of discomfort – it was all a matter of manual skill, and Eddie certainly had that. His brief tried for a plea of diminished responsibility, and said his client was apt to do crazy things on a combination of Daprisal and alcohol. But the plea didn't work, and Eddie suddenly did a turn-around and confessed to the murder of Laura Bingley, too. Unfortunately, we couldn't prove that one, so it had to be ignored.'

Eddie Lawrence was convicted of the murder of Cynthia Hambleton and was sentenced to 20 years in prison.

Sitting in the public gallery throughout the trial was Esther Grant. She was saddened to know that no direct justice could be handed out on behalf of that poor waif of a girl whose face still invaded her dreams. It had been a great relief, nevertheless, to hear Eddie Lawrence speak up and admit that he had killed Laura. At least, Esther said, she would sleep better now – and so, she believed, would Laura.

The Spectre

International archives of forensic psychiatry are full of cases
where men and women have suffered such deformities of
personality that even their basic instincts have failed to con-
form to the general human patterns. This was certainly the case
with a petty criminal from Amsterdam who seemed to turn,
within an alarmingly short space of time, from an indolent thief
into a brutal murderer. For nine weeks during the late 1980s
his crimes spread terror across a wide area of Holland until he
was identified, tracked down and proved beyond doubt to be a
cold-blooded killer, thanks to the combined investigative
efforts of a police detective and a forensic pathologist.

The case began, as far as the law was concerned, in the early
hours of 11 November 1988. A middle-aged couple, Cyriel and
Betti Teirlinck, came home to their bungalow on the southern
outskirts of Amsterdam to find that the back door had been
forced open. When Cyriel tried the light switch he found that
the power had been cut off. The couple came to the same swift
conclusion: they had been burgled. A wave of minor burglaries
had persisted in their neighbourhood for weeks in spite of the
vigilance of police and civilian patrols.

Cyriel groped his way to the hallway to reach the telephone
so that he could call the police. As he moved from the kitchen

79

into the hallway his wife, a few steps behind, saw a dark shape move out in front of him. Before either of them had time to react, Cyriel had been struck on the head with a walking stick from the hallstand. As he fell backwards the attacker moved behind him, pushed his head forward and cut his throat with a long-bladed knife.

Cyriel fell to the floor. The attacker threw himself at the full-length glass panel of the front door, shattering it, and made off across a wooded area at the side of the house.

Betti's screams brought neighbours running and within minutes the police were on the scene. A paramedic team was too late to save Cyriel, who had bled to death in less than ten minutes. Electric power was restored and scene-of-crime officers moved in. As the paramedics turned their attention to Betti and treated her for shock, one man waited patiently to speak to her. He was Inspector Louis Buysse, a specialist investigator from Amsterdam's homicide bureau.

'It was the second murder scene I had visited that night, and only half a mile away from the first,' he said. 'They were two terrible deaths. One young woman, Benita Elsschot, and one middle-aged man. Both had had their throats slit, and both had apparently surprised a burglar. Except there didn't appear to have been any burglary – breaking and entering, yes, but nothing taken. As far as I could see from a superficial look at the way the intruder worked, both these crimes had been committed by the same person, and it looked very much as if he had simply broken in and lain in wait for his victims.'

A computer check by radio telephone drew a blank: no such *modus operandi* was currently on record. 'Crimes like that are worrying as hell,' Buysse said. 'They're not committed by ordinary thugs and clowns who are out to gain at someone else's expense and accidentally kill somebody in the process. They are committed by head-cases who want to kill, and apart from the extreme dangerousness of such criminals, the fact that they're strangers to their victims makes them damned hard to catch. There are simply no lines of attachment to follow.'

The forensic pathologist who examined the bodies was Frank Gezelle. He confirmed that both victims had been killed by the same assailant, and he further noted that the knife had been wielded with some precision. 'To be sure of killing someone with a cut-throat attack,' he said, 'the best thing the assailant can do is to get the knife in contact with the neck, then force the head down, so that the skin is slack across the throat. Otherwise, if the chin is raised and the skin of the neck is taut, the carotid bundle – the group of great vessels which carry so much vital blood – moves back into the protection of the sterno-mastoid muscles, and therefore only the larynx is likely to be cut. This assailant, in both cases, deliberately forced the head down so that there was ample access to the major blood vessels as the knife slid through the skin across the front of the neck. Death in those circumstances is practically assured. This murderer knew precisely what he was doing.'

Inspector Buysse found himself focusing on the forensic evidence as it accumulated. He had a feeling, he said, that if this killer was ever caught, only the clues he left behind would catch him. No amount of deductive thinking was likely to impede an individual who simply wanted to kill other human beings, regardless of who they were.

Five days after the Amsterdam killings, on a lonely stretch of road near Beverwijk, a man carrying a shotgun and wearing an anorak and woollen ski mask climbed in through an unlatched window at a farmhouse and crept up the stairs to the main bedroom. Asleep inside were Willem and Fran Nijhoff, a young couple who had been given the old farmhouse as a wedding present by Fran's parents eight months earlier.

Willem Nijhoff was awakened by the creaking of the bedroom floorboards. He reached out and switched on the bedside light. The masked man was standing at the foot of the bed, pointing the gun. Willem roared at him to get out of his house, and as he moved to get out of the bed the man in the mask fired the gun. The shot hit the upraised duvet. Fran Nijhoff woke up and screamed. The gunman turned and ran out of the room. As Willem stood up beside the bed he realised he had been wounded in the forearm. Clutching his arm, he ran out of the room after his attacker, but by then the man had gone.

'He had left some traces of himself behind, however,' Inspector Buysse said. 'The ribbed pattern of a shoe sole was found on the lino floor covering in the kitchen, and the mark of the instrument he had used to ease up the window was the same as the mark left on the door at the Teirlinck house in Amsterdam. There were also red fibres, a mixture of wool and some synthetic material, which had caught on a rough edge of the bedroom door as he made his getaway, and these matched several found at the homes of both murder victims in Amsterdam. We were glad he hadn't killed anyone this time, of course, but the presence of a gun in the scenario was worrying. All signs of a variation in method are a worry when ordinary motive is absent.'

The police decided they could only wait for the killer to strike again, since there were no clues to make the basis of a manhunt. 'And that wasn't easy,' Buysse said. 'There is no tension more nerve-tearing than the kind felt by police officers as they wait for a potential killer to give in, again, to his appalling urges.'

The man the police wanted to catch was Karel Hensen, born in Amsterdam in 1953, the son of a well-known radio comedian. Since earliest childhood Hensen had been encumbered with a variety of physical and emotional defects which put him at a distance from other children. When he was eleven his parents died in a skiing accident and because there were no other relatives he was put into the care of the local authority. Karel grew into puberty as a weak, introverted and uncommunicative boy; he was held back even further by a stammer, although it disappeared for no apparent reason when he was sixteen. At school he had a low retentive capacity and seemed to understand very little. When he left school he could not read, write or do even the simplest sums.

Before he left school Karel became involved in petty crime, but he was as inept at theft and burglary as he was at everything else. Consequently he made a number of appearances in court. In time, however, through mixing almost exclusively with criminals and by committing the same kinds of crime over and over again, he became proficient at petty theft and minor burglary and had several spells in prison.

Karel had never had a proper job and never sought one, so he had a lot of free time. He used some of it to teach himself to read properly, and the rest was spent living rough in the countryside, often for weeks at a time. He became skilled at field and survival crafts. Between his various jail sentences, and until he was finally unmasked as the notorious Spectre, his talent for survival and concealment often came in handy.

Along the way Karel developed an abiding interest in killing. As a small boy he had watched animals being killed in sheds at the back of butchers' shops and at the local slaughterhouse; later, while he was a prison inmate, he had been shown photographs of a judicial beheading in Peking. Gradually, he built up a collection of photographs of people being put to death in countless bizarre and horrible ways, and he possessed six videotapes, bought from Amsterdam porn dealers, which purported to be 'snuff' movies. (They were not even convincing fakes, but Karel said the simulation of killing 'soothed' him.)

In 1973, when he was twenty, Karel worked as a casual labourer on a city building site, and during that time he carried out a number of burglaries, usually during his lunch break. On one occasion, while he searched the drawers in a lavishly furnished dining room, he was disturbed by the owner of the house, an old man with a walking cane. Karel said that as he stood looking at the frail old person the possibility of killing him presented itself strongly as an option. For a long moment he thought he was going to do it, but at the last minute he turned and ran from the house.

Back at work, he couldn't shift the mental image of the silent, outraged old man standing in the doorway, confronting a much younger man who could have killed him as easily as breaking a dry old stick.

'The idea was like having a strong drink,' he told a prison psychiatrist. 'It distorted the control I had over my senses. I wandered about the building site doing the wrong things, nearly having accidents, all sorts of crazy things happening just because I couldn't get over the idea of having the chance to kill somebody and not taking it.'

Three days later, Karel went back to the house and made a deliberately clumsy and noisy job of breaking in. He went from room to room, rattling open drawers, banging doors shut behind him, but all to no avail – there was no one at home. Two days after that he went back again and this time he found the old man asleep in a chair. Karel took a heavy knife from his belt and stood waiting. The old man woke up and started to get out of the chair. Karel held himself back, waiting until the man was really agitated, his heart pumping hard. Then he swiped the blade of the knife across the wattles of the wrinkled throat.

'Blood just spouted out of his neck,' Karel said, 'and when he tried to make a sound, tried to howl or something, blood shot out of his mouth too. Then he fell back into the chair and I watched him just fade away in front of me. I saw the life going out of him.'

The experience reverberated powerfully for Karel over the ensuing weeks. A month after the first murder, he committed a second. The victim this time was an eighteen-year-old girl, a waitress in a hamburger restaurant. Karel had walked in through the open back door and stood in the kitchen, his knife drawn, just waiting for someone, anyone, to walk in. The waitress was the first, so she was the one he killed, pulling her head well down as he had read in a commando combat manual. On that occasion the impulse had been particularly strong and the outcome was doubly soothing – always the word he used – because the girl wore a white blouse and the entire front of it turned crimson in less than a minute.

'She dropped to her knees on the tiles,' Karel said, 'and she hugged her arms round herself, not touching her neck. Her eyes were all glassy, her mouth was moving but not making any sound, and she rocked back and forward and the blood kept pouring out of her neck. After a while she just fell over backwards and I ran out of the place.'

In the aftermath of the two murders Karel began to wonder why he hadn't been caught. He had taken no special precautions to cover his tracks or to falsify his identity, as thorough criminals were supposed to do. He had failed to do it and yet he had come to no harm. He decided, after some thought, that his determination must act like a cloak. 'I had heard that these things go by opposites, and I think it was probably true. If I kept being bold about the way I worked, I wouldn't be caught. But after two murders I lost the feeling for it. I didn't want to do it any more.'

In 1974 another man confessed to the two murders Karel had committed. Karel followed the case in a state of bemusement, not sure how he should feel. The man had set up a false trail so skilfully that his story was believed; he was tried and eventually went to jail. Once inside he became very withdrawn and eventually committed suicide.

When Karel heard about the suicide he was incensed. Until that time his feelings had remained in suspension, leaving him largely unaffected. But now there was no doubt, he was angry. Not only had the man stolen his crimes from him, he had died and put himself beyond the reach of Karel's revenge. 'So I told myself that one day I would do it again. Not long after that, at the beginning of 1975, I was caught and charged with fourteen burglaries. I did them all – I didn't bother to deny it – and I got twenty years in prison. That delayed things, but I still swore to myself that when I was a free man, I would start killing again, and this time I wouldn't stop.'

Karel was released from prison after serving twelve years. In the autumn of 1987 he set about rehabilitating himself, which meant getting a small apartment, a job, a modest second-hand car and a near-by stretch of countryside where he could live rough should it become necessary. After a year of re-acclimatising to life on the outside, he celebrated his new existence by going out and killing Benita Elsschot and Cyriel Teirlinck.

No psychiatrist ever offered a satisfactory explanation for Karel Hensen's obsession. Killing 'soothed' him, he said, but he would not agree that it was a particular thrill, or that he got anything in the region of a sexual kick from the crime. He displayed no signs of an active sexual instinct of any kind. 'He appeared to be entirely asexual,' said an examining psychiatrist, 'and if that was not really the case, I certainly could not prove otherwise. Neither could anybody else, so far as I know.'

After the incident at the Nijhoffs' farmhouse, where he had planned to watch someone die of gunshot wounds, Karel reverted to carrying only a knife. He now believed that the gun was a potently unlucky symbol for him, and was not appropriate to the type of killer he was. In the true psychotic tradition, he believed he had stumbled on something that worked counter to his 'vibrations'. He felt he had had a lucky escape.

His next victim was a young female naturalist who lived in an elaborate old gypsy caravan, parked at the edge of a wood in Aalsmeer, near Hilversum. For a few days Karel watched her through binoculars from a hide he had built almost a mile away where there was room for both himself and his car.

When he had established the naturalist's pattern of behaviour – he felt it was important to know that, although he could not explain why – he drove down to the caravan one evening, shortly after dark, and parked among the trees a short distance away. He waited until the lamp inside the caravan was doused, then he got out of the car and used a screwdriver to break open the door.

The young woman heard him breaking in and was halfway out of bed when Karel grabbed her. He pinned her to the wall with her head pulled forward and drew his knife sharply across her throat. He then relit the lamp and knelt beside her as she bled to death. He did not leave until he was sure every sign of life had gone from her body.

'The murder was discovered around noon the following day,' said Inspector Buysse. 'Again, I watched the forensic clues being gathered, and I became so caught up in the notion that a murder scene contains all the necessary evidence to solve the crime that I found a clue of my own. Sixty feet or so from the caravan the forensic people had spotted tyre marks, but when I went to have a look it was the shrubbery that caught my attention. Down about knee height, maybe a little higher, a couple of stiff little branches were broken off sharply, and on the pointed tip of one was a pale blue metallic fragment, no bigger than a fleck of paint – and that was what I reckoned it was, a piece of the paintwork of the car that had left the tyre tracks.'

While Buysse was having the fleck of blue material analysed, Dr Frank Gezelle was making an interesting discovery on the body of the latest victim. 'Scratches and bruising around the face and shoulders suggested there had been a struggle,' he said, 'and during the struggle the side of something that looked like a screwdriver had been pressed against the dead woman's arm, just long enough and hard enough to make an impression which left a well-demarcated bruise. I wouldn't have sworn to it at the time, but it looked very much like the shape of the implement that had been used to force open the caravan – and the door at the home of the Teirlincks, at Benita Elsschot's place, and the window at the Nijhoffs' farmhouse.'

As the forensic technicians made casts of the tyre marks near the caravan, they found a faint but sharply defined sole print of a shoe. It was ribbed and looked like a match for the print found at the Nijhoffs' house. 'The usual thing was starting to happen,' Buysse said. 'We were getting a lot of nicely interlocking evidence, all of it pointing to the same person, but we didn't have a damned clue who he was.'

Meanwhile, a microscopic examination of the tiny sliver of material found on branches near the caravan confirmed that it was paint, and although the specimen was too small and too thin for an analysis to be made, three chemists were prepared to say that the sample was entirely consistent with the metallic paint used on motor cars.

In another laboratory, photographic technicians were able to reproduce the shade of the paint and print out samples on shiny paper to emulate its metallic gloss. These were circulated to car dealers in the hope that somebody could put a name to the shade and indicate the particular vehicles on which it might have been used.

Then the killer struck again. This time he broke into a flat in Bussum and attacked an elderly retired lawyer he had been watching for three days. The old man was asleep in a chair when Karel Hensen grasped him by the hair, forcing his head down, wielding his knife in the other hand.

But a big, sudden surprise was in store for Hensen: his superstition about guns was about to be confirmed. The old man pulled a tiny .380 Colt Mustang pistol from the pocket of his smoking jacket and shot Karel point-blank through the shoulder.

Panicking and terrified, Karel hit the old man, knocking him out of the chair, then ran out of the flat clutching his shoulder. 'I went straight to my own flat, driving one-handed,' he said later. 'Once I was inside I locked the door and got out my US Marines survival manual. I flipped to the section on emergency operations. It showed me how to get a bullet out of myself, and frankly the sight of the pictures, and the instructions on what I had to do, nearly made me faint. But I was in such pain anyway that I went ahead. It made a terrible mess, but I managed it, I got out the bullet. Then I irrigated the wound with alcohol, and after that I burned the edges with a lit candle. Some time after that, while I was trying to clean up, I passed out. I think I was unconscious, on and off, for three days.'

At first, the police did not connect the attack on the retired lawyer with the Spectre, as the killer was now known, thanks to a scare campaign in the press. Buysse was alerted when he read a report by a junior detective of the old man scaring off an attacker with a knife. 'Frank Gezelle, the pathologist, got very interested too,' Buysse said. 'He was working up his own profile of the killer, and when he saw on my report that the lawyer had shot the attacker at point-blank range, he was anxious to get a look at the gun. I told him it was still at the lawyer's house, and Gezelle went rushing round there himself to collect it from the old man.

'By the time I got to the city mortuary later that night, to chew over the case, I found both the pathologist and the lawyer sitting on opposite sides of a laboratory bench discussing the implications of a batch of analytical test results they were waiting for.'

Gezelle explained that his excitement was to do with a forensically useful phenomenon that occurs when some handguns are used at close quarters to human targets. 'The

Colt Mustang is one of the weapons it often works with,' he said. 'The effect is known as "back spatter". A contact shot will sometimes cause blood and fragments of tissue to enter the muzzle of the gun, and they sometimes travel a fair distance along the barrel. It's caused, I believe, by a suction effect that occurs when the blast gases subside and there is a sudden cooling in the gun barrel.

'Fragments of all kinds can get sucked in there – hair, skin, bone. In this case, the suction effect had indeed occurred and I swabbed blood, skin and clothes fibres out of the Mustang. We sent them for full analysis, and the lawyer was able to use his influence to get extra-special priority, so the results were with us the same evening.'

The most practical result of this testing, from an investigative point of view, was the blood grouping, and the fact that a quantity of that same blood could be shown to have mingled with the fibres of a specific kind of cloth from the assailant's shirt. 'As the case now stood,' Buysse said, 'just as soon as we knew who this man was, we could bury him in evidence that told us practically everything but his name.'

Three car salesmen told detectives that they were convinced the particular shade of blue of the paint found near the Aalsmeer caravan was the one used on Peugeot 205 models. There were hundreds of that shade throughout Holland. Nevertheless, Inspector Buysse told his men to be on the lookout for a Peugeot 205 of that colour, possibly with a scratch along its side at approximately knee height.

'These cases always work out anti-climactically,' Buysse said. 'Two days into the search, an officer found a car that was the right colour, the right make and right model, and yes, there was a scratch along its right-hand side at roughly knee height. It was parked on a quiet street not far from Amsterdam city centre.'

A watch was put on the car, and at a distance of 200 yards its front tyres were photographed. The pictures were rushed to the central police laboratories and given speedy treatment. Within twenty minutes it was confirmed that these tyres were the ones which had left imprints in the ground near the caravan where the naturalist was murdered.

While Buysse and two other officers continued to watch the car, Karel Hensen emerged from one of the terraced houses and stood by the car fumbling for his keys. Buysse and another officer got out of their car and hurried across. They stood one either side of Karel, their hands almost touching behind him in case he decided to run for it.

'Is this your car?' Buysse asked him.

Karel hesitated, then said yes, the car was his. Why did they want to know?

'We have reason to believe you could help us in our inquiries into a number of serious crimes.'

Karel looked from one man to the other, and then to their surprise – and his own, as he later admitted – he sighed and said, 'I think I can do more than just help – I can solve the lot for you.'

In the end, everything tied together with a degree of neatness that Inspector Buysse had rarely seen in a criminal case. Screwdriver marks on property and on the arm of one victim matched exactly a screwdriver found in the boot of Karel Hensen's car. The fibres, shoe print, blood and skin specimens were all proved to have come from one source. 'We had the Spectre nailed to the wall,' Buysse said.

The defence at Karel's trial had to go for a psychiatric plea, claiming that Karel was not definably sane. The judge agreed with that, but he reminded the jury that the defendant was not an imbecile, however deformed his mind might be. He certainly knew right from wrong.

The jury concurred. Karel Hensen was jailed for life on three counts of murder, with no recommendation of a maximum term. It is not expected that he will ever be released.

A Matter of Chance

On a frosty morning in December 1980, a man walking his dog across common ground in Leek Wootton, Warwickshire noticed a hummock in the grass by the edge of a skaters' pond. It had not been there the previous morning. Ice crystals glinted on the small mound as the man approached, and when he came within five yards of it his dog darted forward and began running round the object, sniffing and barking. Up close, the man saw that the thing on the ground was the body of a child, a girl, curled in a foetal position, with thick frost on her face, hair and clothes. The man backed away, frantic, beginning to shout, scaring his dog and making it bark louder.

Two hours later a small, bewildered-looking woman, Lucy Davidson, stood in the anteroom of a hospital mortuary, waiting to view the body found by the frozen pond. Her eleven-year-old daughter Irene had been missing for seventeen hours, and the description of the dead girl – light brown hair, hazel eyes, wearing a brown anorak, a grey school skirt and a Fair Isle jumper – matched Irene's.

A policewoman stood close behind Lucy as she was brought to the side of the sheet-covered trolley. An attendant lifted the end of the sheet, Lucy gave a small cry and the policewoman caught her as she slumped. Later, when she had recovered sufficiently to hold a cup of tea and listen to gentle questioning, she told a detective that Irene had gone out to play with friends just after teatime the night before, about half-past five. It had been dark, but their cul-de-sac of modest, privately owned houses was well lit and there were always plenty of people about.

'It always seemed safe enough,' Lucy said.

None of the children could recall seeing Irene after six o'clock. One girl said she believed she saw her wandering along the road on her own, but she couldn't be sure; another said she thought Irene had gone chasing off after a puppy which had appeared under one of the lamp-posts.

'The usual thing had happened,' a detective said. 'Kids had played and then they had gone in for the night, and none of them really had any idea what had gone on outside of their own small sphere. They genuinely racked their memories, but none of them had been playing with Irene that evening, so none of them had any real idea about her movements. All we could say with any certainty was that she had died, possibly from suffocation, and that her body had been dumped by an unknown person on common ground a few hundred yards from where she lived.'

At the post-mortem examination, because smothering was a common finding in cases of this kind, the pathologist was careful to look for signs that would suggest there had been pressure on Irene's face. As expected, there was bruising on the insides of the lips, caused by unusually firm contact with the front teeth, and that suggested that sustained pressure had been applied to her mouth.

'Nothing violent, though,' the pathologist recalled, 'which isn't to say that force wasn't used. But it was done with some gentleness, so as not to do any damage that was externally visible. If a person is strong enough, and patient enough, he or she can put a hand over a weaker person's nose and mouth and just keep it there, and in time that person will succumb to anoxia and eventual death from the reduction of oxygen to the lungs.'

There was no evidence of sexual interference, and there were no marks on the body or clothing to suggest a struggle. The pathologist's guess at the time was that Irene had been held motionless, unable even to struggle, while a gentle, firm pressure over her nose and mouth kept her from breathing.

'While there was no external bruising on the nose or mouth,' the pathologist said, 'I was aware of a smoothness, a difference of feel in the area, so I took swabs and some skin scrapings and sent them for analysis. I also noted that there was a scent of something like rose water from the stomach contents. That was also unusual enough to make me bottle some samples for the analysts.'

The police began house-to-house inquiries around the cul-de-sac where Irene had lived. Questioning the adults, they did not receive the customary response in such cases: neighbours tend to say that a dead child was popular and bright, loved life and was liked by everybody. On this occasion, however, a few parents on the street said Irene had been surly and ungregarious, and only ever went out among the other children in order to criticise them. 'I had trouble keeping my face straight,' said a policewoman. 'One old dear said, "Irene was a miserable little bugger, God rest her soul," and her neighbour told me the only time the girl smiled was whenever another kid got hurt.' Nobody appeared to have disliked Irene actively, but most people who knew her remarked how temperamental and cantankerous she could be.

'But the Evans lad liked her,' said one interviewee, Howard Brough, who lived in the largest house on the cul-de-sac which sat squarely on the curve at the top. Brough was a retired bank manager, now a semi-professional entertainer who did a cabaret conjuring and mind-reading act. 'I can see right down to the main road from my lounge window,' he said, 'and being here most of the day, I have a good idea of what goes on. The Evans lad was definitely keen on young Irene.'

Brough was asked to expand on what he meant by 'keen'. He said that Brian Evans, a seventeen-year-old who worked in a local branch of a chain of newsagents, used to come to his gate at night and talk to Irene if ever she was about. 'She wasn't all that jolly as children go,' he said, 'but that didn't seem to deter Evans.'

A similar story was told by Violet Drew, a forty-six-year-old accountant who lived alone in a house at the opposite end of the cul-de-sac, near the main highway. 'I got the feeling she came out on the street after school to hang about and wait for the Evans boy to show up,' Violet said. 'She didn't come out to play with the other kids, she was too cheerless a kid for that.'

The detective in charge of the case, Bill Mason, decided to interview Brian Evans himself, telling his parents that he was trying to enlist another young person's slant on the day-to-day movements in and around the area. He could see the mother did not believe that. Mason spoke to Brian in his own room. 'If you feel you have to,' his mother said acidly.

From the outset the interview was hampered by the distractions of Brian's decor. He had a number of light-emitting electronic devices he had designed himself, and explained to Mason that they operated on the impulses generated by the human voice, just like disco lights responded to the base beat in music. 'I found it heavy going, but I resisted the urge to ask him to turn them off,' Mason said. 'I was trying to avoid any negative tone at all, because I didn't want him tightening up on me. Suspects who aren't tense or defensive tend to let things slip more readily. That's what I believe, anyway, and I always work on that assumption. The lad appeared pretty relaxed as we talked, but the flashing and blinking lights, all different colours, were bugging me to the point that I don't think I was responding to things as sensitively as I might have.'

After a few general questions about the cul-de-sac's population, the children who played there regularly and the people from other areas who came and went, Mason asked Brian if he knew Irene particularly well. Brian shrugged. He had known her, he said, but he wouldn't say he knew her well. She was not very communicative, he added. She spent a lot of time standing and staring.

'I tried various ways of pressing the point,' Mason said. 'I asked him if he was well enough acquainted with any of the kids that they would wave if they saw him in the shop where he worked. He said yes, so I asked him then if Irene had ever waved to him at work. He said no. But I kept doing that, talking about the kids in general and then narrowing it down to Irene in particular, not worrying too much if he thought I was suspicious of him. I was more concerned that I should seem to have a pattern to my approach, which, again, reassures people – even guilty people – and makes them less likely to protect themselves against slips.'

After a while Mason looked up at the wardrobe and noticed six photograph albums set in a row on top. He asked Brian if he could have a look. Brian nodded, but he looked uneasy. The detective took down the albums and opened one. It was full, from end to end, of pictures of children. The shots were technically accomplished, mostly in black and white, and most of them depicting the children from the cul-de-sac playing their games on the pavements and in the road. 'This is a good place to photograph kids,' Brian volunteered. 'No traffic's allowed into the road. It means they play all over the place, and other kids come to play with them, so there's always plenty of them to shoot.'

Cautiously, Mason asked Brian if taking pictures of children was a particular enthusiasm of his. 'Along with other stuff,' Brian said, pointing at the five albums on the floor by Mason's foot. 'I like photographing anything, as long as there are people involved. My instructor says I like photography the way gluttons like food.'

'Your instructor?'

At college, Brian said. He attended evening classes and was working for the Intermediate Certificate of the City and Guilds, after which he hoped he would get a job in a professional studio.

Mason looked through the other albums. One was devoted to photographs of men working in an engineering factory; another was all women – nurses, policewomen, lollipop ladies – also at work; the third and fourth showed activities at local judo and karate clubs, and the fifth contained portraits of Brian's family and people at the shop where he worked.

Bill Mason believed he had drawn a blank. He thanked Brian for his time and went back to the station, where he wrote out a report for his superior. The next day, within an hour of the report being delivered to the DCI's office, Mason was called in and asked, rather coldly, if he had not considered it odd that two separate witnesses from different parts of the area where the murder victim had lived both said they thought Brian Evans had enjoyed an unhealthily close association with the dead girl.

'The boss said there had to be some reason for that, some reason for two people to observe a particular closeness, and even if Brian Evans did seem like an upright chap, a healthy hobbyist, he should be pressed further, and harder, on the nature and depth of his relationship with Irene Davidson.'

Mason went back and spoke to Howard Brough. He asked him if he was absolutely sure that Brian Evans had shown a partiality towards Irene, given that he liked taking pictures of the children anyway. 'It wasn't pictures he had in mind,' Brough said darkly.

Mason noticed that as he spoke, Brough handled a large

coin, bobbing it from hand to hand, rolling it between his fingers the way conjurors do. He saw the detective looking at the coin and he explained that it was his lucky silver dollar. 'I believe in luck. This piece is my talisman. Everybody should have one.'

'You said it wasn't pictures Brian had in mind,' Mason prompted, getting back to the subject. 'What does that mean, exactly?'

'I've seen it in young men all my life. I've witnessed it even when I was a child myself. The intense type, often quite young himself, hanging around near the younger girls and getting fixated on a special one. I'll tell you candidly, Officer, the way he looked at that girl, it made you want to turn aside and not think about what was happening.'

That evening, when Violet Drew got home from work, Mason called on her. He asked the accountant again whether she was sure there was something special in the way Brian Evans approached Irene. She repeated that it was unmistakable, and that she could detect something deeply unwholesome in the youth's regard for the little girl. At that point she said something else which, for Mason, recast the whole perspective of the investigation. He wrote down her words, as he had written down Howard Brough's. Then he thanked Violet for her time, and left.

He went straight to see the pathologist and asked him if he would mind going over his findings again. Once more the medico-legal facts of the case were set out. The girl had died of suffocation. There were no marks of violence on her body, but a slickness of the skin around the mouth and the external nasal area had prompted the pathologist to take swabs and skin scrapings. Nothing else exceptional was found, except for an oddly out-of-place scent of rose water from the stomach contents, which otherwise appeared to be ordinary part-digested food.

'While I was there,' Mason said, 'the pathologist called the laboratory to ask if there was any result on the analysis of Irene's stomach contents. They said not yet, but the swabs from the mouth and nasal areas showed a positive presence of zinc stearate. I'd never heard of the stuff, but the pathologist told me it was a compound of zinc oxide with variable proportions of something called stearic acid and palmitic acid, used as a specially smooth dusting powder.'

Mason was now deeply unhappy about the case. He had half-formed suspicions which were too shapeless to suggest a line of direct inquiry. He knew he should start driving hard at Brian Evans, setting aside considerations of the young man's feelings, so that the underlying truth of his relationship with Irene Davidson could be made clear. But to Mason that felt like taking a possibly harmful line along a route he did not need to follow. 'I wouldn't have admitted it at that time, but I was convinced by then that Brian Evans had nothing to do with the murder,' he said. 'Believing that, I didn't want to bruise his view of the authoritarian world any more than I had to – he was, remember, a forward-looking, productive and eminently sane member of society, and I don't believe in tampering with the brains and emotions of people like that, especially when there are so few of them.

'So I tried to think of another way of approaching the whole thing. I looked through the meagre bag of clues we had and decided that, thin as they were, I would use them, if it was at all possible, to establish my line of inquiry.'

Mason plodded around all the retail chemists in town, inquiring about sales of zinc stearate, or *zinci stereas*, as they insisted in calling it. Nobody had sold any for years. He decided to try further afield, in Stratford-upon-Avon, and found one pharmacist who had sold three ounces of the chemical less than a year before. He did not know who had bought it, for although it did require a signature in his poisons book, the book in question had been one of a number of items destroyed by drug addicts who had raided the shop.

'They do that,' Mason explained. 'They get into a chemist's back room at dead of night, thinking they'll steal all the drugs in the place, and then they discover that chemists know by now that drug-heads do that kind of thing and the schedule drugs are all in big metal cabinets like safes and can't be got at. So the intruders trash the place.'

The next thin clue was a chance remark by a neighbour of the Davidsons, who had said that Irene did seem to get on well with little Eva, a seriously handicapped nine-year-old with cerebral palsy who was sometimes brought to the gate in her wheelchair so that she could watch the other children play. The neighbour had said Irene was openly solicitous to Eva and had even made her a special mobile for her bedroom. Coming from a child like Irene, the neighbour added, that was an act of extreme affection.

Mason had already seen Eva, and had not considered it worthwhile trying to interview her: apart from the possibility of distressing the child, it did not look as if she would be able to give articulate replies to his questions. Nevertheless, he was determined to follow the clues as far as they would take him, so he called on Eva and her family, not at all sure what questions he wanted to ask.

Eva was a huge surprise. She had control of one leg only, and the rest of her body appeared to be in a perpetual chaos of conflicting movement; her head swung from side to side and her eyes rolled, she drooled and squealed between bouts of grunting sounds. Everything about the child appeared unstrung and hopelessly random, yet within twenty minutes Mason was talking to her, increasingly unaware of her handicap. Even her speech, which at first sounded garbled, became easy to understand when he realised that the vowel sounds were all extended and the consonants were rushed. 'It was a dialect. It was no more exceptional than that. All you had to do was listen, and the longer I listened the easier it got.'

Mason asked Eva if Irene had spoken much to her. Yes, Eva said, she had; she treated her exactly as she would any normal person (only better, her mother put in). Had Irene said anything about anybody she didn't like, Mason asked, anyone she really didn't get on with? Eva told him Irene did not like the other kids much, they were too childish. But as for not liking anyone in a personal way, the only one Eva could think of was somebody called Paranor.

Mason was puzzled. Paranor? Had he picked it up correctly? He asked again and Eva, with a great deal of effort, repeated the name. Paranor. She did not know who that was, but Paranor was a pest, Irene had said it a couple of times when she was complaining about her school, and where she lived, and how she would like to go to another town.

After a while it occurred to Mason that he was making Eva tired. He apologised, thanked her for her help and left. On his way home, he tried out the name Paranor several times and decided that the pest called Paranor might be an object rather than a person. It seemed likely that another clue had led him nowhere.

At home there was a message on his answering machine. It was from the pathologist. The rose-water aroma he had detected came from Turkish Delight, he said. One of the chemists had recognised the scent, and checked the chemical analysis with a specimen from a local shop.

'It's the expensive kind,' the pathologist added. 'Imported.'

Mason called at the Davidson house and asked Lucy if she had bought Turkish Delight recently. Not at all, she said; she didn't recall ever buying it since it was a confection she didn't particularly like.

Before turning in for the night Mason decided that, although none of the clues had led him in any direction, he would still have to address his unformed suspicion, the one that had made him change his view of the case in the first place. And he would have to do it cold, without the flimsiest evidence, let alone anything concrete.

The next morning, before he had time to plan his moves, there was a call from the chemist in Stratford-upon-Avon. He had mentioned the matter of the *zinci stereas* to an assistant, and she had recalled who bought it: 'It was a local accountant, she has an office around the corner from here. Miss Drew, Violet Drew.'

One up to forensic science, Mason thought. Now his unformed suspicion was promising to take shape. He looked again at his notebook, at the two pieces of statement that had made him wonder. One was from Howard Brough, when he talked about Brian Evans hanging around Irene Davidson: 'It made you want to turn aside and not think about what was happening.' The second was from Violet Drew, on the same topic: 'It made you want to turn away and not think about what he was up to.'

Now, with one clue, the zinc stearate, tying the two people together, Mason admitted the sharpest of suspicions: collusion. And they had cooked up their story without proper attention to detail.

Before leaving the station Mason called a friend in an analyst's laboratory in Birmingham and asked him what people used zinc stearate for nowadays. A dusting powder, the friend told him, though not much, since it was toxic. Magicians still used it, though, he added. 'They rub it on their playing cards, it turns them very smooth, and makes it easier to do those showy fans conjurors like making.'

Mason went straight to his boss and told him what he now had: two people who seemed independently to finger the same suspect, but used similar language to do it, and now they were apparently connected by the purchase of a powder, traces of which were found on the mouth and nose of the murdered girl. 'What you have here,' his boss told him, 'is called, I believe, an epiphany.'

Mason found Howard Brough at home. He asked if he could come in, and when he was shown into the ornately furnished sitting room, the first thing his eye settled on was a large box of Turkish Delight. Imported.

'And the second thing I clocked was a conjuror's table,' Mason said. 'On the cloth apron that hung down at the front, the word "PARANOR" was stitched in gold sequins.'

Brough saw Mason looking at the table and told him that Paranor was his stage name; it was based on the word paranormal. He was chattering nervously, Mason noticed, so he did nothing to interrupt the flow.

'I like to encourage people to use that name, rather than my real one,' Brough said, 'because spreading the name can only publicise the act, which is all to the good . . .'

Mason asked him if he encouraged children to use the stage name.

Brough's façade began to wilt. He set his teeth, Mason noticed, as he tried to hang on to a smile. To the best of his recollection, Brough said, he had never encouraged any children to use his stage name.

'And does Violet Drew help publicise your act?'

It was a pleasure, Mason said in retrospect, to watch a bad man come unglued. Brough looked down at his hands, clenched them, stuffed them in his pockets and looked at Mason. He seemed suddenly distraught. He swallowed a couple of times, then, in a shaky voice, he demanded to know what Violet Drew had been saying about him.

'I think we know enough,' was Mason's reply, which he hoped was enigmatic and menacing enough to make Brough confess. And he did – though not in an entirely direct way.

'You have to understand something,' he said. 'You have to understand it before anything else gets said here. Some of these kids, these innocent little children, are animals, no other name for them. They can be downright evil.'

At that point, Mason admitted, he was thinking on his toes. 'Why did Violet Drew go along with it?' he said. Brough did not understand, so Mason tried another tack. 'She wasn't put off by the way you feel about little girls. Why's that?'

Brough looked at the window for a moment, then said that he would like to have a solicitor to represent him. Mason said that would be arranged, and he drove Brough to the station. However, when they arrived Brough changed his mind. He seemed almost anxious to make a statement and get it over and done with.

He said he had invited Irene Davidson into his house a couple of times and pretended he wanted her to train as his little assistant. He even had a costume made, which he wanted her to put on. All he wanted to do, he swore, was see her put it on, to watch her as she did that and to be near her as she learned to handle the props. He had no plans at all to touch her. He was quite simply a man who took pleasure in looking at children, at certain children . . .

Violet Drew loved him, he said, and in his way he loved her, although they continued to be discreet after his wife died, just as they had been before. That somehow added an edge to the relationship. Brough had confessed his penchant for looking at certain little girls (certain little boys, too, as it transpired), and Violet Drew had found no difficulty in accepting that – she had a couple of weaknesses of her own, which she hoped that Brough, in his turn, would accommodate.

'The girl had said nothing to her parents about visiting me,' Brough told Mason, 'but even if she had, I was prepared to approach them and go through with the little deception, having her train as a magician's little assistant . . .'

105

It was Brough's belief that the girl knew the nature of his true feelings for her, and the evening she died, when she had wandered close enough to the house to be beckoned in, she had behaved, as he put it, 'coquettishly', agreeing to come in, but being surly once she was there. One thing had led to another – he had *so* wanted to please her – and he had found himself kneeling before her and putting his arms around her. She had struggled suddenly and begun to shout. He held her gently, he swore it, only trapping her, keeping her from running away, putting a hand over her face to keep her from making a noise. Then suddenly she was limp, and he realised she was dead.

'Violet helped me, she calmed me in the end. We disposed of the body after the place was quiet. Then we decided that if we were asked, the boy with the camera, Evans, would be singled out as a likely culprit. Neither one of us likes him.'

Some time later, when Brough had been charged with Irene Davidson's murder and Violet Drew had been charged as an accessory, Mason called at the Evans house and asked to speak to Brian. He wanted to know if the lad had any idea why Brough and Miss Drew might have disliked him. He wanted to know because neither of them would say why, yet on reflection he had realised they must have disliked Brian very badly to consider pinning a murder on him.

'Yes, I think I know why,' Brian said.

He went to a chest of drawers, took out an envelope and handed it to Mason. There were three photographic prints inside. They showed Violet Drew, at various stages of being led out of the newsagent's where Brian worked, a police officer on either side of her. In the third shot she was openly glaring at the camera.

'Shoplifting,' Brian said. 'They kept it out of the papers, but she came into the shop and warned me she would do me a lot of harm if I ever let anybody see the pictures, or if I ever talked about what happened.'

'But you've hung on to the pictures, anyway?' Mason said.

'Souvenirs,' Brian said, putting them back in the envelope. 'Imagine . . .' He shook his head. 'A snobby, toffee-nosed woman like that, getting done for shoplifting, and now she's been had up for helping a murderer.'

'Just a couple of her weaknesses, I suppose,' Mason said.

When Howard Brough was remanded in custody, he spoke briefly to Bill Mason as they waited for the van which would take him to the remand centre. Brough still had his lucky dollar, which the guards had said he could keep with him. 'You maybe think it didn't do me much good,' he said to Mason.

'I don't think anything about it one way or another,' Mason replied. 'I don't place any faith in the notion of luck. Life's all down to chance.'

Brough said that Mason was entitled to believe that. It had been a matter of chance that Irene Davidson had died, and a matter of chance that he had been handling his cards before she entered his house; that was Brough's view of chance, he saw it as a black happenstance.

Luck was the opposite of chance. And the lucky dollar, the talisman, would see him through, he knew it would. 'And you'll know it, too,' he told Mason.

That night Howard Brough died in his cell at the remand centre. He had poisoned himself. His lucky dollar had in fact been a magician's device, engineered from two silver dollars made to look like one, half of it a push-fit lid, the other hollowed out to make a circular box. It was opened by applying pressure to a spot on the rim. Violet Drew revealed that for years the coin had carried Brough's escape route, in case he ever found himself in a position where he could no longer decide where he would go next or what he would do. One gram of potassium cyanide, swallowed in a second, killed him within another four.

A search of Violet Drew's property produced a lipstick case with a false decorative top: she too had a gram of potassium cyanide, the gift of freedom from her lover. But she had not had the courage to use it. Instead, she spent two years in prison for being an accessory to the concealment of an act of manslaughter.

A Thoughtful Man

The retirement homes provided for elderly people in
Dordrecht, south of Rotterdam, Holland, were regarded by
the authorities as a milestone in the humane approach to
resettling widows and widowers. So many old people, finding
themselves suddenly alone in the world, were either unable to
cope with maintaining a home on their own, or required
somewhere much smaller, because their need for space and
their physical ability to manage it had diminished.

'The retirement village was an attempt to provide citizens
with support without encroaching too severely on their independence,' a former supervisor recalled. 'Each little house had
a living room, a small kitchen, a bedroom and bathroom, all
within a neat space that managed to avoid being cramped.
They had small back gardens, too, which were tended by
contract gardeners. In essence, they lived their lives like any
other citizens, with the additional safeguard of supervisors on
site, providing patrols three times a day, discreetly checking on
them, making sure everything was all right.'

The village, which consisted of three parallel streets of
twenty such houses, was the focus of much attention at its
inauguration in 1959. Similar 'sheltered' schemes were piloted
in America and in Great Britain, all of them owing an

acknowledged debt to the basic design and administrative concept of the Dutch project.

The first death at the Dordrecht village occurred in 1961. The deceased, oddly, was the youngest resident, a sixty-three-year-old woman who had regularly gone for long walks and made a point of helping other less mobile residents. She was found dead in a chair in the small living room, the radio playing softly on a table beside her. The supervisor recalled that the woman's death was a great shock to her son, who had been planning to take her on holiday. 'He was distraught. He could not understand why a woman who had never been ill a day in her life could so suddenly die, with no prior warning, and at such an early age.'

Because the dead woman had not needed to see a doctor, her medical record was not adequate to provide reasons for a cause of death, so a post-mortem examination was ordered. The pathologist found her cardio-vascular system to be in good shape; she simply appeared to have suffered a 'gross insult' to the system, which the pathologist tried to explain as an invasion by an unspecified agent which caused the heart to stop. It was a very unsatisfactory cause of death, because it offered nothing of how or why the woman had died. But the pathologist had no more to add.

Another death occurred ten days later on another street: this time the resident was old and infirm, a man of eighty-six, found, just like the woman, sitting in an armchair, facing a blank wall. This time, since the man had a record of cardio-pulmonary disease, a death certificate was issued by his doctor, giving chronic heart failure as the cause of death.

'Perhaps if there had been a delay of months, or even weeks, before the third death, no suspicion might have been aroused,' said Dr Piet de Mattos, a forensic pathologist in Rotterdam at the time. 'But ten days after the second death there was a third. This one was a man of seventy-two, again found in a chair in his little house, apparently a natural death just like the other two. But the general feeling was that this was too much for coincidence.'

There was no immediate suspicion of foul play. The village administrators had an emergency meeting and decided that there might be an intermittent gas leak, or some other source of airborne poisoning. Experts in gas technology and others who had investigated the wartime effects of buried chemicals were brought to the scene and for a month there was complete disruption as gardens and whole roads were dug up in an effort to locate a concealed, unspecified menace.

'And I, meanwhile, had to try to find what exactly had happened to the three people who had died,' de Mattos said. 'The bodies of the woman and the second old man were exhumed and laid out in their putrefying splendour on tables on either side of the freshly dead victim. I was young and extremely keen in those days, and as I recall, my enthusiasm left no room for disgust at the state of the bodies that had been buried – the woman's was particularly bad. I had a challenge on my hands, and I had all the resources of forensic science lined up behind me, ready to help. That was how I envisaged my position. I still had idealism in those days.'

Because there was a suggestion of gas being involved in the deaths, de Mattos looked very carefully for signs of toxic invasion by carbon monoxide. 'I had catered for the possibility of ordinary, through-the-mouth-with-liquid poisoning by sending specimens of blood and stomach contents to the laboratory,' he said, 'and one or two other possibilities were being handled by the lab people. Usually with carbon monoxide poisoning, there is striking evidence right on the surface, on the skin, which turns a cherry-pink colour, but in two of the cases before me the skin was every shade except pink, and in the third it was the standard dead white. That did not exclude the possibility of gassing, of course. So I opened up the bodies and proceeded with the examinations cautiously, taking notes all the way.'

The most noticeable internal feature of carbon monoxide poisoning is, again, the cherry-pink colour, in the blood and in the muscle, caused respectively by carboxyhaemoglobin and carboxymyoglobin. No such signs were found in any of the three bodies. The laboratory was asked to make blood tests for low levels of carbon monoxide, while de Mattos cut sections of the three brains and looked for degeneration in the basal ganglia, which are four masses of grey matter located deep in the brain's hemispheres.

'I found nothing unusual,' he said. 'So I began looking on the surface again and I came across a curious coincidence. On the body of the third victim – the seventy-two-year-old man – and on the woman, I located patches of diffuse bruising on the backs of the wrists. Because the woman's body was decomposing badly I had to use filtered light to look at the wrists, but the bruises were definitely there, and on both people they looked very much alike. It was a definite finding, in the forensic sense, so it was reported.'

Fred Coenen, an inspector with the Rotterdam police, went to the mortuary to have a look at the bruises. Coenen had seen hundreds of violent crimes in his career, many of them murders, and he believed he knew what had caused the bruising. He had seen it on victims of bank hold-ups, kidnaps and rapes. 'It is usually caused,' he said, 'by the hands being restrained with the heels of an attacker's hands.'

He could remember a case where a patient in a hospital bed had been given a poisoned drink by a nurse, who then leaned down on the backs of the wrists with the heels of her hands to restrain the patient's struggling, until it subsided and he died. 'It is not so much a technique as an instinctive manoeuvre,' Coenen said. 'The one thing an attacker has to do, in so many cases, is control the flailing arms and hands of his victim. If it's done with the elbows, spread outwards and pressing down sideways, it leaves practically no mark at all. With the heels of the hands, though, there's always a mark, and nearly always the mark looks the same.'

So now there was the possibility that two of the dead people had been physically restrained at some time prior to their death, and both in the same way.

The clues stopped there. Test results from samples of blood and stomach contents came back showing nothing unusual. Further dissection of the brains of the three bodies failed to show any changes apart from those of a degenerative nature, which were to be expected in view of the ages of the dead people, especially in the cases of the two men.

'The street-digging stopped and all the holes were filled in,' the supervisor recalled, 'and everything was put back as it had been. A great deal of expense and disruption had been incurred and nothing was found. People began living their normal quiet lives in the village again, and the three who died were laid to rest, two of them for the second time. Everything went back to normal.'

And then, incredibly, another of the residents died. An old woman in her early eighties was found in a chair by the window, her face placid and normal, so much so that the first patrol of the day had waved to her, thinking she was looking out of the window. When she was still there, looking the same, when the second patrol went past, the officers investigated. There were bruises on the backs of this person's wrists, too. As soon as Fred Coenen heard that he set up a full murder investigation.

'I couldn't wait until they were all wiped out,' he said. 'We were chasing nothing more substantial than the supposition that a killer existed, but we had to act, we had to try to be at least a barrier to this happening again.'

Two days after the fourth person died the daughter of the

second victim called at the supervisor's office and said that, on going through her father's belongings, she had discovered a significant financial discrepancy. 'That was not how she put it,' the supervisor recalled. 'She said some bastard had robbed him. He kept his money at the house – it was a matter of independence and we could understand that, but right at the start we made it clear that we took no responsibility for the special security of money and valuables. The individual tenants of the houses had to take care of that themselves.

'We got in touch with the relatives of the other people who had died and asked them to check carefully through such records as there might be to see whether there was anything missing. In each case money had disappeared, and the relatives could demonstrate the disparity to our satisfaction, too. In the case of the first victim, the sixty-three-year-old woman, her son nearly went mad. He hadn't even bothered to check his mother's belongings, he had been so distraught at her dying. Everything had been put in a spare room and ignored until the pain of her loss subsided. When he checked, at our request, he found that the present-day equivalent of about US$5,000 [approximately £3,333] was missing.'

If the deaths were murders, at least there was a motive. Fred Coenen did not doubt they were murders, even if, so far, natural causes had been the only official finding. He set up an interview room on the site of the retirement village and interviewed everyone who had business at the site on a day-to-day basis. He also ran extensive background checks on all the people he interviewed.

'It was red-face time for the administrators,' Coenen said. 'Of the six patrol officers employed there full time, three had police records, and one of the other three had fake papers – he was a refugee from the southern USSR. The head gardener was a convicted child-molester, which I supposed was all right, since the retirement village was probably the safest place for him to work – certainly a lot better than up at the children's hospital. Other people such as the milk delivery man and the postman were vetted carefully and cleared.'

At approximately that time a diversion occurred: two old men were found dead at separate pensioners' hostels in Rotterdam, and an examining physician reported that one of them had bruises on the backs of his wrists. 'It was the kind of thing you hope won't happen,' Coenen said. 'You have a spate of killings, and if you haven't a clue what happened you can still be glad they're restricted to a particular area. It gives you a comforting illusion of containment. When they start to spread your heart sinks.'

Forensic technicians visited the scenes of both deaths and collected samples of dust, hairs and fibres; they bagged up all the clothing they could find and took it back to the laboratory for thorough examination. Both bodies were taken to the mortuary and again Dr de Mattos began a meticulous investigation, looking for any irregularity at all. In the case of the fourth person to die at the village, he had again drawn a blank. He had, however, found something vaguely interesting, though not in any obvious way suspicious. Now, examining one of the old men, he found it again.

'It was a transparent greasy smear, hardly discernible, on the cheek,' he said. 'I had found a similar smear on the fourth body from the village – the old woman had one on her chin. It was distinctly oily to the touch, and there was a vague scent, although I couldn't place it, and nor could anyone else around the mortuary. We sent a swab of the first one for analysis and it was still at the lab when I found the second. So we sent that off, too, and told the police we had something else for them to fret over.'

The analysis of the smears revealed that they were Methyl Salicylate, better known as oil of wintergreen. It is used as a flavouring agent, mostly in medicines, and also in salves as a counter-irritant, most commonly in the treatment of chilblains and to ease rheumatic joint pain.

'It was not a promising line to follow,' Coenen said, 'but we had to try to find out whether an intruder had left the smears behind. No wintergreen or preparations containing wintergreen had been found at the scenes of any of the six deaths. Nothing of the sort had been detected on the first three bodies, although only one of them had been fresh anyway. In a curious way, this *did* have the outside promise of a real lead, because it was only intermittently present, which is the profile for so many recurring significant clues.'

While de Mattos worked hard to unearth more clues before the latest bodies were surrendered for burial, Fred Coenen tried to find out just how hard it would be to run a check on the retail outlets for wintergreen preparations in and around Rotterdam. He discovered that a check on customers for the products would be impossible, because practically every corner store sold the stuff, and even a check on retailers could not be guaranteed comprehensive.

'I was beginning to prepare myself for the possibility that these cases would go unsolved,' Coenen said. 'We had six deaths, all of old people, and all of whom – including the two latest, we now knew – were robbed of money. Yet although robbery is a prominent motive for murder, and is certainly behind a vast number of manslaughter cases every year, we had no evidence to say that these people had been murdered, or even accidentally killed. We had no proof that they had died in any way other than naturally. The bruises on some of them could have been plain nothing, just incidental minor trauma unconnected with anything that would interest the police.

'On one level I suppose I could console myself that the case was just too damned difficult, too lacking in evidence to lead us anywhere, but on another I knew perfectly well that the deaths would bother me for years, I wouldn't be able to put them from

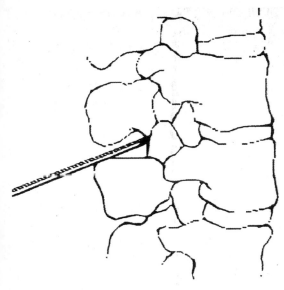

Bird Man: A drawing Eddie Lawrence carried in his pocket, showing the correct angle of entry for the spinal needle.

The Spectre: The primitive hovel where Karel Hensen lived rough in the weeks prior to killing Cyriel Teirlinck and Benita Elsschot.

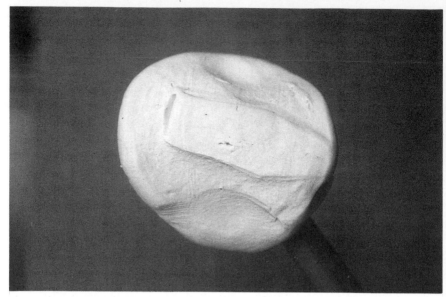

Plastic impression of tool mark from the naturalist's caravan door.

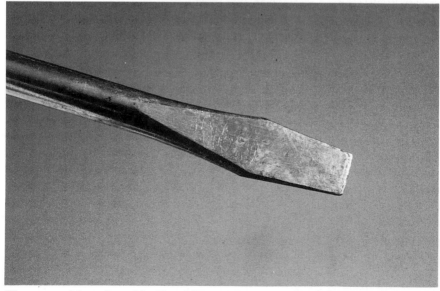

The screwdriver found in Karel Hensen's car matched the impression from the caravan door and other scenes of crime.

The mechanism of 'back spatter'. Pressure from the bullet pushed the skin into firm contact with the weapon; as the muzzle rapidly cools, blood and fragments of tissue are drawn into the gun barrel.

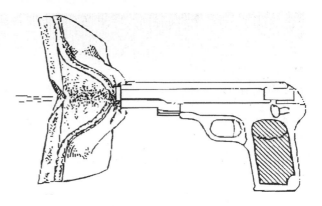

The 'shrinking wound' paradox. Perforation of the skin occurs when the skin is stretched; when it springs back the wound is consequently smaller than the bullet. Around the wound is a ring of abrasion, caused by the bullet rubbing off the top layer of cells while the skin is perforating.

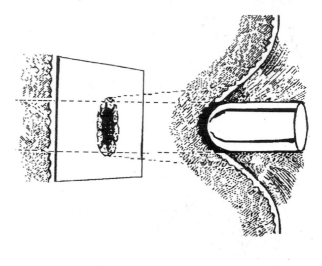

Forensic guide to skin markings in cases of close-quarter shooting. 1: Ring of abrasion; 2: Ring of debris from gun barrel; 3: Powder grains; 4: Powder smoke deposit.

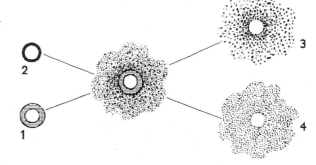

A Matter of Chance: Howard Brough's lucky silver dollar, showing chamber.

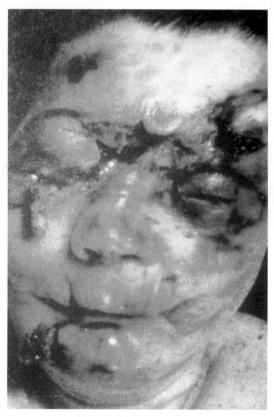

Beneficiary: A pathologist described the attack on Lily Dale as 'ferocious'.

The maggot is .25 inch long, the same length as the pupa. The downward protrusion at the narrow end of the maggot is the jaw hook.

Calliphora maggot | transverse section (20x) | pupa

my mind. Not unless the mystery was solved somehow.'

Another old man died, this time in a long-stay convalescent home. His death might have been certified in the ordinary way by a physician, except that in this case the family doctor was aware that recent deaths of elderly people in Rotterdam were not regarded, by the authorities, as being all that ordinary.

'At the post-mortem I could hardly believe it when I came across another smear of wintergreen,' said Dr de Mattos. 'It was on the left cheek, and because I was looking for smears now, its presence was so obvious to me that I could almost suspect somebody had planted it there in a crude attempt to divert me from something else.'

Fred Coenen did the only thing he could think of: he re-interviewed everyone connected with the village in the hope that he or his officers would detect the presence of wintergreen on somebody. In two cases, there was a suspicion of the distinctive aroma. 'We felt like idiots,' Coenen said, 'getting in a huddle and comparing notes about the smells given off by people. But that was all we could do, and the consensus was that the milkman and one of the window-cleaners both had the appropriate odour. So we got them both back in for intensive questioning.'

The window-cleaner invited serious suspicion when he refused to say anything without a legal representative being present. When a lawyer was summoned he was required to do nothing, because the window-cleaner then provided himself with excellent alibis: first, he never entered the houses in the village (it was in his contract), and secondly, he was always visible to witnesses when he was on the estate.

'It was true,' Coenen said. 'The man was never out of the sight of at least four witnesses at any given point on his rounds. When I asked him casually about the wintergreen he wore, he told me it wasn't wintergreen. It was a eucalyptus preparation for his arthritic shoulder, and he would be happy to furnish proof of that, too, if there was any need.'

The milk delivery man, Jan Minne, was well-liked in the village, because of his sunny temperament and the way he helped people. He took letters to the post office for the ones who had difficulty walking, mended fuses, changed lightbulbs and had even oiled a few squeaky gates. The supervisor of the village described him as a thoughtful man. When he sat down opposite Fred Coenen in the supervisor's office, which had been commandeered for the interviews, he smiled warmly.

'I told him I was sorry we had to keep asking questions like this,' Coenen said, 'and he shrugged, smiled again and looked perfectly relaxed and acquiescent. So then I changed the mood quickly and said I had reason to believe he knew more about the deaths of the six old people than he would so far have had us think. When I said that, I swear he looked so hurt he made me feel like a bastard.'

Without saying that Jan Minne was under suspicion for something so trivial as using – or apparently using – wintergreen, Coenen pointed to the multiple opportunities the milkman had for entering people's homes, knowing where they kept things, gaining their confidence through helping them. And the victims had all lived alone, in places where there were no regular intrusions by other people; even the old man in the convalescent home had been in a room of his own. 'A person in your position, I told him, could do just about anything he wanted in one of those cottages and get away with it.'

Jan Minne agreed that the proposition was feasible. But did the detective, he asked, really think he was the kind of man to do something like he was suggesting – kill old people for their money?

'You tell me,' Coenen said.

And Jan Minne did. He said he was the man they had been looking for, and he said that he was glad he had been caught, since he could think of no other way he could have stopped.

'After the first one I killed, who was strong – I deliberately tried it out on a strong one to see how it would go – I knew I would get into the habit. I get a habit for everything that gives me particular pleasure, Inspector.'

Fred Coenen said that thinking back to that interview, he still remembers the cold sensation in his stomach as he realised he was talking to a psychopath. Jan Minne was still smiling, still relaxed, looking only a little regretful. Coenen asked him how he had killed his victims. Minne reached into his pocket and pulled out a folded square of something that resembled very thin silk. It was a membrane, Minne said, taken from the body of a large species of sea-ray which swam in the waters off Vietnam.

'He unfolded it, and it got quite large, and when he had it all laid out flat on the desk I could see it was fashioned like a bag, rounded at one end. He told me it was completely impermeable. Nothing could seep through it, thin as it was. His brother had brought it back from Vietnam when that country was called French Indo-China. The membrane was an instrument of silent murder.'

The bag was designed to be dropped over a victim's head as he slept. It was so thin that it clung to the lines of the face, cutting off most of the air, and that happened almost at once.

'The effect, de Mattos told me later,' said Coenen, 'is cardio-inhibitory, which is to say the sharp dip in the supply of oxygen causes the heart to stop, and it happens much more rapidly than it would in ordinary suffocation.'

Minne dropped the bag over the heads of people who were asleep, which was the way the device was meant to be used. Even the hale and hearty woman, his first victim, took a nap in the morning, just after her walk around the town. Two or three of the old people made feeble attempts to get the hood off their heads, he added. He simple held down their hands until their hearts stopped, which was all the faster because they had used

119

up their available oxygen making the small struggle.

'They would not really feel anything,' he assured Coenen. 'The struggling was just a reflex. It meant nothing. It didn't mean they were distressed. I would never have done that to them.'

So was it done solely for the money, Coenen asked, or was there anything else?

'The money,' Minne said, nodding. But then he shrugged, indicating that there was more. Coenen waited. 'Maybe the pleasure of doing it, too,' Minne said. 'Maybe that made me do it as often as I did. Being there when they died was a very moving experience. I felt proud I could make that happen.'

He added that he had moved his base of operations to Rotterdam after he saw the upheaval he had caused at the village. He had been planning to put some of the money he had stolen to good use by going to live in Amsterdam, where he firmly believed he could have gone on 'quenching lives' without ever being caught. Not, he added, that he believed, deep down, that that was a good idea. 'I admire restraint, but I've got to have it forced on me.'

After Jan Minne had been charged, Coenen asked him if he used wintergreen. Yes, Minne said, all the time. He had suffered from rheumatism since his twenties and he rubbed it on his aching knuckles, wrists and elbows every day.

'It was the wintergreen that caught you,' Coenen said.

'I hoped something would.' Jan Minne smiled. 'The stuff's even better than people say it is. Don't you think?'

Beneficiary

Late on the morning of Saturday 18 July 1970, Sarah Loudon, a health visitor, telephoned the police in Bradford, Yorkshire, and asked if they would come to a small flat at a council development near the village of Baildon. She was worried that one of the patients on her list, an elderly widow, might be dead.

Sarah explained that two days earlier she had called to see the patient at an agreed time, but had got no reply. Since the old lady, who was called Lily Dale, suffered from angina and never left the flat for long, her absence had been worrying, but Sarah had finally assumed that there must be some good reason, since neighbours thought they had seen Lily not long before. There was no reply today, either, and this time the health visitor detected an ominous smell of decomposition when she opened the letterbox to call to the woman. From the outside at the back of the flats, it looked as if a kitchen window had been forced open.

The police broke into the flat and found the body of Lily Dale on the living-room floor. Her skull had been broken by a blow on the forehead with something hard and blunt. She had obviously been dead for some time. The visible parts of the body had turned green in patches, there was a powerful odour of decay throughout the flat and when the body was moved, a large number of maggots fell on to the carpet.

Mrs Dale had been robbed. An old cash-box – a sister-in-law confirmed she kept her savings in it – had been broken open and lay empty on the living-room floor. Various items of jewellery were also missing.

Lily Dale's bachelor son Albert, thirty-eight, was visited at his home in Bradford and told of his mother's death. 'He was evidently saddened by the news,' a police officer recalled, 'but he took it stoically enough. I remember he said that Yorkshire had become a jungle, and that nobody was safe. It was a typical remark for a man like that. He was rather stodgy, lots of fixed opinions, a bit out of step with things. It was obvious in the way he dressed: tight early-sixties clothes, the haircut, the slim-Jim tie, just his whole appearance and manner.'

Albert said he could not think of anybody who would attack his mother: 'She was liked by everybody. Everybody. It's just been some mindless little burgling bastard who's hit her when she caught him, right? I bet that's what you'll find when you look into it.' As Lily's closest surviving relative, Albert joked that he would probably be sole beneficiary of her will, if they ever found one: 'I daresay there'll be the price of a fish supper in it for me.'

The forensic pathologist confirmed that the blows to the head had caused Lily's death. 'The frontal area of the skull was shattered, and there was what we call a pond fracture along the side of the skull: that's a kind of dent, with little fractures radiating out from the bottom of it in this case. Both areas of injury produced corresponding brain damage immediately beneath them. The attack must have been ferocious.'

Two days after the body was found, one of Lily's friends, another widow called Betty Herbert, approached the police and told them she believed Albert might have something to do with the murder. She added that she had given the matter a lot of thought before she decided to approach the police. 'I would have come sooner,' she said, 'but I was laid up with bronchitis for nearly two weeks and I couldn't get on my feet.'

A police inspector, Cynthia Abbott, spoke to Betty and took a statement. She asked when Betty had last seen her friend. Neighbours at the flats where Lily had lived said they had seen her two or three days before she was found, but it was now clear that they were mistaken.

'I saw her three weeks ago,' Betty said. 'If I'd not been in bed I would have been round to see her a week ago, then maybe this wouldn't have happened, who can tell? Or at least I might have found her – how long had she been dead?'

Abbott said that the pathologist believed Lily had been dead for six or seven days before she was found. She urged Betty to tell her what she knew about the relationship between Lily and her son.

'I've known Lily since we were both young married women. We used to share all our worries and woes, no matter what they were, and we both felt it did us good, having somebody to blow off steam to. I never had any kids and Lily had only the one, that Albert, and he was a bad little sod right from the time he could toddle. You can see the badness in some kids from the time they're little, and he had it to spare. He's been a burden to Lily all these years, not the blessing a son should be.'

Abbott pressed Betty to be specific and tell her something more about her suspicion that Mrs Dale's son had something to do with her murder.

'This past eighteen months or so Lily was forever telling me how she'd been having rows with Albert about money,' Betty said. 'It was money she'd lent him and he hadn't paid back. Hundreds of pounds, she reckoned.'

Abbott was naturally wary about the testimony. She tried to find out if Betty Herbert had any special reason for disliking Albert Dale beyond her instinctive aversion – an unstated grudge, perhaps. Betty admitted she had very little time for the man, but that was only because she'd had so much affection for Lily, who had been so callously used by Albert.

'He never had any real feeling for Lily,' Betty said. 'She had to admit that herself, finally. If he ever came near her it was to scrounge money, or a meal he was too lazy to make for himself, or anything else he needed and couldn't get easier elsewhere. Lily reckoned sometimes he just took things, without asking her. He even took the batteries out of her torch once. Can you imagine that? Lily saw him fiddling with the torch out in the hall and asked him what he was doing with it. He told her he was adjusting the spring in the switch because it wasn't working right. Next time she went to use it for going out the back to the bin, the batteries had gone.'

Abbott asked if Lily had made any recent mention of the money arguments between herself and her son.

'She talked about it last time I saw her,' Betty said. 'She told me he kept on at her for more, instead of trying to pay back some of what he owed her. She said instalments would have been all right, she just wanted him to show willing.'

Albert was questioned by a CID officer, who asked him about borrowing money from his mother, and about any arguments they might have had because of it. Albert flatly denied ever borrowing from her. He told the police Betty Herbert was a nosy old cow who made up stories out of malice. 'Besides that, the pathologist said Mum was probably killed some time the previous Saturday, Friday at the earliest, right? Well, I went to Amsterdam on Tuesday of that week and I didn't get back till the next Monday. She was killed while I was away.'

Albert's story was checked. He had, indeed, been away on shopfitting contract work in Amsterdam since 7 July, and had not returned to Bradford until early on the 13th. It had been estimated that Lily Dale was murdered on the 10th or

11th – the 11th seemed most likely. Albert's alibi was logged and the focus of the investigation shifted to a group of young offenders already suspected of aggravated burglaries in the area.

The forensic pathologist who performed the autopsy on Lily Dale had already wondered, in retrospect, if he might have made a mistake. When he heard about Albert's statement he decided to look at the whole matter again. 'I had based my original estimate of the time of death on the state of decay of the body,' he said. 'Gut bacteria had broken down the haemoglobin, resulting in green staining in the abdomen, which usually takes eight or nine days in conditions such as those in which Lily Dale was found.'

Now he began to take account of the fact that, although it was summer, it had been a cold July in Yorkshire. According to the police, the heating at Lily's flat was programmed to come on for an hour in the morning and two hours in the evening, with the thermostat set to create an ambient temperature of 24°C. That created a factor which had been taken into account when the pathologist made his estimate of the time of death.

'I could have let it stand, of course, because I had acted on the available evidence, and no one would have faulted either my procedure or my findings. But I have to say that when I was shown the interview notes with Albert Dale I had a very unscientific feeling that he wasn't half as clean as he was presenting himself to be. So, in the sneaky, suspicious-minded tradition of good detective work, I decided to back-check everything, starting with the central heating at Lily's flat.'

The police were slightly put out at being asked to check on the heating timer again, but they did, and they confirmed the settings. The pathologist asked them to *try* the settings to see if the apparatus was working. They did that, and found that although the timer was accurate to within two minutes, it appeared to be no longer capable of turning the heating on or off.

A call by a detective to Betty Herbert confirmed that the heating timer had been broken since the spring; she gave the detective the name of a private heating contractor who had installed systems for a number of elderly people in the area, and he said he had been waiting months for a replacement part to repair Lily Dale's faulty switch.

'So Lily's body had been lying in a cold flat,' the pathologist said. 'Which meant she had probably been dead a lot longer than I had estimated. It was no use simply revising my estimation of the time of death, however; I needed an estimation with solid scientific clout behind it. I had a suspicion that the maggots might provide a clue, but since my knowledge of the flying invaders of dead flesh has always been shaky, I enlisted the help of an experienced entomologist.'

Dead specimens of maggots from Lily Dale's body were sent to Dr Beryl Tranter, a forensic entomologist based in Leeds. 'The idea,' she explained, 'was that if I could work out the age of the dead maggots, I could then give an indication, based on their stage of development, of the minimum time Mrs Dale had been dead when she was found.'

Estimation of a time of death based on the development of maggots can be relied on only if the body is cooled soon after it is discovered, otherwise the maggots will go on maturing. In the case of Lily Dale, the body was placed in cold storage two hours after it was found. Dr Tranter found that the commonest maggots in the collection were those of *Calliphora*, the blue-bottle (in this case *Calliphora Erythrocephala Meigen*, the most common variety in the UK). The life-cycle of this creature is very well documented.

'You will often hear police officers who attend the scenes of murders or other unexplained deaths mention the fact that there were blowfly maggots on the body,' said Tranter.

'Blowfly is the colloquial name for a group of flying insects called *Diptera*, which are found in practically every country in the world. They include the bluebottle, the greenbottle and the common housefly. From a forensic point of view, one important feature of these insects is the fact that their life-cycles are altered by climatic conditions.'

Another significant fact is that bluebottles do not fly in darkness, so their eggs are laid only in daylight hours. Hence, in any body found at night or in the early hours of the morning with fresh *Calliphora* eggs on it, death almost certainly occurred the day before.

'The eggs are very distinctive,' Tranter said. 'They're yellow and banana-shaped, and the bluebottles prefer to lay them on fresh rather than decayed flesh. They lay them very soon after death, or even on living people or animals, too, if the targets in question are in some way debilitated by wounding or sickness. One bluebottle will lay anything from 300 to 2,000 eggs in little clusters of 50 to 150, always on moist areas like the eyelids, nostrils, mouth, genitals and anus. They go for open sores too – maggots often show up in leg ulcers.'

Since the development of *Calliphora* maggots is closely related to surrounding temperature, a twenty-four-hour monitor was set up in Lily Dale's living room. The weather had been reasonably constant for several weeks so the resultant temperature range of 7°C to 15°C was taken to be an acceptably accurate basis for calculations.

'It had been anything but warm in the flat,' Tranter said, 'so the development of the maggots would have been slow. The eggs won't hatch below 4°C, but they certainly will between 6° and 7°. At that point in the investigation I had to start examining the dead maggots carefully, looking for various signs such as the slight thickening of the outer covering that develops when the ambient temperature is relatively low. That and other factors, such as sectional appearance when they were cut in half, gave me a good indication of their rate of development.'

The stage in the life of an insect between periods of moulting is called an instar. At the first instar stage the maggot tries to eat through the skin of its host, or enter into any near-by body cavity. To aid this, the maggot exudes strong proteolytic enzymes which break down proteins or peptides in a process which is virtually identical to digestion. This first instar lasts for about eight to fourteen hours. In the case of the maggots found on Lily Dale, Tranter found signs which indicated that the first instar stage had lasted nearer twenty-four hours.

'And the following stages were similarly extended,' she said. 'I could easily demonstrate this from a number of factors such as the density of the skin on the maggots, their colour, their length and mean weight – all these factors add up to an indication of how long the insect has taken to develop.'

The second instar stage lasts on average two or three days. In this case, Tranter was sure it was nearer five days and took the trouble to consult other authorities in Germany, who agreed. 'The estimated time of Lily Dale's death was getting further and further back from the original estimate of 10 or 11 July,' she said. 'What I was looking for in the final stages of my own estimation was some sign of mature third instars, the kind that are often found remote from the dead body, looking for somewhere to hide while they pupate. When I looked at several of the maggots under a low-power microscope, I could see that they were uniformly white in colour, indicating that they were fully fed. In other words, they had stopped eating the corpse and their intestines had cleared.'

In Lily's case the shortest time within which maggots in this stage of development would show a clear intestine would be ten or eleven days. The uniformly white maggots were at the end of the third instar stage and had begun moving away to pupate elsewhere. The revised estimate seemed more and more likely to be the time Lily's body had lain in the flat before it was found.

'So, going back ten or eleven days from the time the body was found, we came to Tuesday 7 or Wednesday 8 July,' Tranter said. 'Albert Dale had not left for Amsterdam until late on 7 July.'

So Albert's alibi had gone. The police examined the evidence, and spoke at length to Dr Tranter and to the pathologist who had set the new investigation in motion. They also talked to the forensic scientists who had examined the jemmied window at Lily's flat and had now decided it had been forced open from the inside. In the opinion of the officer in charge of the investigation, the new findings strongly suggested that the police should return their attention to Albert Dale. A search warrant was obtained for Albert's flat in Bradford and he was taken in for questioning.

Albert vehemently denied any connection with his mother's death, and repeated his assertion that he had never borrowed money from her. 'What kind of son would do a thing like that?' he demanded. 'I loved my old mum, I wouldn't do anything to hurt her, and I definitely wouldn't borrow money off her. I've seen the time when I was able to help her out with a few quid when she hadn't been for her pension and didn't want to borrow from her nest-egg. A mother should be able to rely on her son for that kind of help, but the other way round – well, it's just not on.'

Albert was confronted with the fact that it now appeared Lily could have died before he went to Amsterdam, and that the jemmied window at her flat looked like an inside job. Albert turned silent for a time, then began to concoct a new, semi-coherent defence. He blamed the murder on his cousin, a hemiplegic: 'He never liked the old lady, he said as much.'

Working strictly by the book, the police brought in the cousin, David, a frail man in his mid-twenties who walked with the aid of a stick. David was told bluntly that Albert had accused him of murdering his Aunt Lily. David said he wasn't surprised; Albert would say anything to save his own neck.

'He's an habitual liar,' David told the police, 'and he's good at it, but sometimes he just goes over the top. If you think I might have done in Aunt Lily, just go ahead and investigate me. But I'll tell you now, it's all I can do to swat a fly without falling over, let alone batter somebody to death.'

The search at Albert's flat had turned up nothing that would incriminate him. The police decided to search the place again, this time using a specialist team for whom house-searching was a full-time job. The officer in charge of the murder investigation was impressed. 'They had only been in the place ten minutes when they found £700 in banknotes hidden in a false waste pipe under the sink, and under it was his mother's missing jewellery wrapped in a duster. Some of the notes were so old they weren't legal tender any longer.'

Counting the money, a detective suddenly realised the significance of a list of numbers he had found at Lily's flat: they were the serial numbers of these same banknotes.

Albert finally caved in and confessed. He had needed cash to repay a £125 gambling debt owed to an aggressive foreman-carpenter on the shopfitting team. Albert was not due to be paid for work he had recently done until two weeks after completion, so there had been no wage packet to draw on.

'He's a bad bastard, that foreman,' Albert said, 'not the kind you can fob off. I owed him and he said that if I went into the game to try to win, I should have been prepared to lose, too. So I had to get the money. He'd have mangled me if I hadn't got it.'

On the morning of Tuesday 7 July he had gone to his mother's place before ten o'clock, since the foreman wanted his money by noon. Lily refused to hand over another penny, and when she tried to stop Albert taking money from her handbag he hit her. She fell down. He picked up an ornamental brass poker and hit her again, twice, killing her.

'I can't say why I did that. It happened. One minute she was alive and making a noise and the next I'd hit her with the poker. No thinking about it, as far as I remember. I just did it, that's all. It got the problem solved.'

He cleaned the poker, used it to force open a rear window to simulate a burglary, cleaned it again, emptied his mother's purse and her cash-box, and left with the money and jewellery.

'When I'd got the debt off my back I felt a bit better, even though I still had a murder to deal with,' he said. 'But after a couple of days, when nobody had found the body, I got calmer and I put together that set-up in the kitchen with the waste pipe. I suppose I should have made a better job of it.'

Having made a clean breast of the crime, Albert asked the police a question: what had made them revise the estimate of Lily's time of death? The interrogating officer told him about the age of the maggots.

Albert made no response to that. Later, while he was on remand, he was overheard telling another prisoner that he believed the police were using a red-hot new method of determining a victim's time of death, but they weren't letting anyone know the details. He didn't blame them for doing that, he said, but he would have thought they would have come up with a better cover story than that nonsense about the age of maggots.

In January 1971 Albert Dale was put on trial for robbery and murder. A jury found him guilty and he was sentenced to life imprisonment.

Love Letters

Nowadays, any bomb small enough to be carried is assumed to be a political weapon, and the main emphasis in the training of explosives experts is on the understanding, handling and dismantling of bombs made by political terrorists. The bomb used on an individual as a means of personal revenge for non-political reasons has never been a common expedient, and in recent times it has become very rare. It wasn't surprising, therefore, that when a bomb went off in a house in the Inglewood district of Los Angeles in the summer of 1986, the police mounted a full-scale terrorist alert.

'You feel so bad about these things afterwards,' said Daisy Yarborough, a neighbour, 'thinking you could have done something, when of course you couldn't – how could you know what's going to happen? But of course even though you know that, it doesn't make you feel any better . . .'

Daisy was sitting on her front porch, knitting, on a warm Tuesday afternoon in July, when she saw the mail delivery truck draw up at the house opposite. She watched idly as the mailman got out, carrying a large yellow padded postal bag. He walked up the path to the front door and rang the bell. The house was owned by Denise Longton, a radio producer, who had lived there alone since her divorce six months previously.

Daisy watched to see if Denise would answer the door; quite often she was out during the day. If that was the case today, Daisy would take in the parcel for her, as she had done a couple of times before.

'Then I saw the door open and Denise appeared, smiling as usual. She took the bag from the mailman. Just before she closed the door she looked across and waved to me. I waved back.'

A minute later there was a tremendous explosion. For a second Daisy didn't know what had happened. Her first thought was that a plane had crashed into the street. Then she saw that Denise Longton's house was shrouded in smoke. Daisy dropped her knitting and ran across the road. As she hurried up the path she heard the noise of falling metal and tumbling glass, then a gust of wind blew the smoke aside and she saw that an entire side wall of the house had been blown out.

'It was just awful,' Daisy said. 'Everything in the house looked as if it had been picked up, hammered out of shape, then thrown against the wall and left to lie where it fell. It was chaos, a smoking and clanking nightmare. And then I saw these clumps of red stuff that had hit the wall and slid down, leaving a scarlet trail, and I realised that they must be Denise.'

An hour passed before the police convinced themselves that there had not been a terrorist attack. They stood by as inspectors from the power and gas companies examined pipes and cables to see if a water boiler or a kitchen appliance had caused the explosion.

'Of course, we knew by then that it was something else, something brought to the scene,' said Lieutenant Ray Bush, who was in charge of the investigation. 'There was the smell of explosive in the house, and that's something you can't mistake, but we had to go through all the procedures, just for elimination. When the boys from power and gas were gone, the explosives expert moved in. He was Luke Matthews, a very experienced man with a couple of fingers missing to prove it.'

Matthews entered the shattered house alone, picking his way through the debris, visualising the outward course of the blast, tracing it back to source. It was not easy, because although an explosion will create distinct lines outward from its core, when the blast is enclosed the shock waves will double back on themselves, creating a whirlwind trail that effectively conceals its starting point. After an hour, however, Matthews was able to say, with certainty, that the explosion had emanated from a point near the rear of the sitting room.

'The area immediately adjacent to an explosion is often the least damaged,' he explained, 'and looking around there, among the smashed wood and glass from a cabinet and a cluster of shattered spotlights, I fished out an empty yellow padded postal bag like the one Daisy Yarborough saw being delivered. I also picked up numerous fragments of notepaper with handwriting on them. The large envelope had only a tear along its back and was otherwise unharmed. In view of the fact that it was delivered a minute or so before the explosion, and adding to that the fact that it was found right at the epicentre of the blast, I decided we were probably investigating a letter-bomb incident.'

The body of Denise Longton was recovered as a series of fragments, twenty-three in all, which were taken to the central police morgue for examination. The pathologist determined, from the shape of certain pieces and the trauma they had sustained, that the main damage had been done after the explosion blew Denise into the heart of the maelstrom of flying glass and metal. 'It was like she'd been dropped into a giant blender,' said the pathologist.

In this case, as in any other, the scene of the crime was the major point of investigation. A team of forensic technicians descended on the quiet street and surrounded the shattered house and its surroundings with tall grey screens. They then set up a grid search. This involved marking off, in twelve-inch squares, an area 150 feet long by 20 feet wide beyond the blown-out wall of the house.

'Then more than fifty technicians got down on their knees,' said Ray Bush, 'and got busy with tweezers, magnifying glasses and collection bottles. They worked every inch of that space, each covering the area of one square at a time, moving on only when a square had been thoroughly searched. Each square was photographed before it was searched, then the pieces of debris were classified, catalogued and put in bottles and envelopes carefully marked with the square each piece came from, and its position within the area of the square. It was a monster of a job, but nobody ever told those guys their work should be easy.'

The first suspect was the dead woman's former husband, Bernard Longton, who ran a bookshop in Vermont. Since the divorce, which had followed a long period of estrangement, Bernard Longton had on a number of occasions pleaded with his wife to let him have the house in Los Angeles. Failing that, he would have settled for living in a rented room there. The set-up in Vermont had turned out to be nowhere near so idyllic as he had imagined, and for three years he had wanted to transfer his business to LA and build up a clientele there.

When Ray Bush showed up at Bernard's bookshop, which was in attractive and expensively furnished premises on the corner of a fashionable street, he had the feeling that Longton had been expecting him. 'The look he gave me was the kind you see on someone's face when their bus finally shows up. I don't think he was pleased to see me, he just wanted to get the thing over with.'

Ray Bush started his questioning by asking Bernard Longton when he had last seen his ex-wife. A week ago, Bernard said, when he had visited Los Angeles and tried yet again to get her to rent him a room in their old house. Bush asked why he had to live there, of all places; there were plenty of other places in LA where a man on his own could live.

'It was for a number of reasons,' Longton told him, fingering his neatly clipped beard. 'Mostly, though, it was to do with picking up on a thread of intent, if you follow me.'

Bush said he wasn't sure he did.

'Well, I chose that house in LA. I singled it out for the atmosphere, the way the light slants across the road at a certain time of day, the view you can get of a sunset from the kitchen window. It was a kind of heartland, I suppose, an inspiring source-place where I had my best ideas.'

So why had he moved to Vermont three years ago?

'I had this feeling, after visiting Vermont a couple of times, that I could make a terrific go of a business up here. Again, it was a matter of atmosphere, the *feel* of the place. LA had somehow drained the colour out of my ideas. The store I opened there had been a success but it was without character – I didn't create the magical, benign *web* I wanted to achieve. To me, you see, a bookshop is a state of mind, and it should impose its special character on a customer.'

Patiently, Ray Bush asked him why it hadn't worked in Vermont. Longton said that the place was right, but the people were worse Philistines than they were in Los Angeles. 'At least in LA they're honest Philistines. Here they dress it all up with literary name-dropping and memorising reviews and lists of books, and recalling the years certain books were published and all the shit. I'm sick of it.'

Ray Bush pointed out that the bookshop in Los Angeles hadn't worked out, either. So why did he want to go back?

'I realise, now, that I had the nucleus of something good beginning to form in LA,' Longton said. 'But I wasn't patient enough to wait it out and let the thing grow. That was a terrible mistake and I've paid for it with three years in this phoney

wonderland. I want to start again in LA; I want to give it the
time it needs. Living in that spot is important to the venture,
because I want to recreate the states of mind I could only
experience there.'

The house, Bush pointed out, was all but destroyed. It
would have to be demolished. He wanted to see Longton's
reaction to that. Longton nodded sadly, shrugged and said he
would never have been able to stay there, anyway. He knew
his ex-wife's heart was set against the idea and nothing he
could have said would ever have changed her mind.

'Maybe, if the land comes up for sale, I could buy it
again . . .'

Bush remembered that Longton looked at him squarely
then, very level-eyed, and said. 'You've come all the way up
here because you think I was responsible for what happened to
Denise – isn't that so?'

'You are a suspect, yes,' Bush said. 'You can surely see that
was inevitable.'

'And is Larry Stuart a suspect, too?'

The name was new to Ray Bush. Research into the dead
woman's background had turned up very few acquaintances;
she worked alone, even keeping herself apart from her produc-
tion team at the radio station, and socially she did not mingle
with many people. That, according to her sister-in-law, had
been one of the reasons behind the marriage breakdown, apart
from Denise's refusal to pull up roots and move to Vermont.
Bernard had wanted to cultivate social contacts and connections in Los Angeles, but Denise would not support him in
that.

'I admit,' said Ray Bush, 'that I didn't want Bernard
Longton knowing that I hadn't a clue who Larry Stuart was, so
I told him, yes, you could say Stuart is a suspect.'

The questioning, after that, followed a stock pattern, Longton pointing out that someone like himself, who was his

ex-wife's only known enemy – although he felt the word was too strong, they had merely disagreed – would have been an idiot to try getting away with murdering her. 'Unless I were the kind who likes being hassled by police, which I'm not.'

Back in Los Angeles, a little research produced the information that Larry Stuart was an art director with an advertising agency. He was married and lived with his wife and three daughters in a modern mansion at Santa Monica, a mile north of Los Angeles International Airport. At the radio station where Denise Longton had worked, only one person, an executive secretary, admitted that she knew that Larry Stuart and Denise had been seeing each other, discreetly, for more than two years.

'So, with all the subtlety and diplomacy for which American cops are famous,' Ray Bush said, 'I barged right into Larry Stuart's office and told him that I not only knew he had been seeing Denise Longton, but that he was as high up the list of murder suspects as it was possible to get without falling off the top. He was a very stiff and formal gent, and he looked at me like I was something that had stuck to the heel of his shoe on the way in. He told me he would not speak with me any further than to ask me to leave. Any questions I might have I could address to his lawyer, and he passed me the man's card.'

Meanwhile, the padded envelope found at the scene of the explosion had been passed for examination to a fingerprint specialist, Peter Weiss. He had removed the address label carefully and handed it over for assessment, together with the fragments of notepaper bearing the handwriting, to a forensic document-examiner. As far as the envelope itself was concerned, Weiss had to decide if it was worth the risk of putting it into a chemical solution that would reveal fingerprints, but which might make the envelope useless for any further tests involving chemicals.

'We couldn't do the other tests first, either, because they

might destroy any latent fingerprints,' Weiss said. 'What I had to decide, really, was whether it was likely that the bag had retained any worthwhile prints. My experience of this kind of packet – it had a smooth, semi-absorbent surface and close-knit fibres on the outer cover – was that it was capable of providing fingerprints of such a fine quality that there would be no difficulty in photographing them and ultimately producing a match, if the same prints were resident in the criminal finger-print database. Of course, on a number of occasions I'd tried to get prints off such a packet and come up with nothing but smudges. A lot depended on the quality of the paper, and in the end you had to trust to the kind of instinct that doesn't explain itself, it just tells you yes or no.'

He decided to go ahead and perform the chemical test for fingerprints. The procedure is standard and is usually referred to as the Ninhydrin Test. A bath is made up containing a solution of the chemical triketohydrindene hydrate, which acts like a developer, bringing up any latent fingerprints on paper in the form of dark, sharp images, rather like photographs.

'And we were lucky. A number of prints appeared, and we were eventually able to eliminate those of the mailman, and those of Luke Matthews, the explosives expert. That left two prints, rather fainter than the others, which had been deposited there by someone who had not, as yet, been identified.'

The address label of the packet had in the meantime been carefully studied by the forensic document-examiner, Don Baker, and he had issued a report on his findings. 'In summary,' he said, 'the lettering used to address the packet had been gone over several times to thicken it, and this has the additional effect of rendering the letters completely anonymous, since any chance of getting a characteristic from a given line is destroyed by the other lines which are present. There was no postage frank mark, so the only hope of a useful clue might come from the label itself, which appears to have been made from a species of drawing paper. An analysis is being sought.'

As for the fragments of notepaper, they were too small to make much sense collectively, apart from appearing to be the remains of a fairly bulky batch of letters. Work was going ahead to try to assemble some of the pieces to see whether a clue would emerge.

Larry Stuart's lawyer was even more testy than his client. He told Ray Bush that if so much as a shred of defamation should attach itself to the process of investigating the movements and motives of his client, then the detective would find himself, *personally*, held answerable. 'And that, as you know, can cost,' the lawyer added.

Ray Bush was not daunted. 'What I possess,' he told the lawyer, 'nobody's going to take the trouble suing me for. I need to know about Mr Stuart's relationship with Denise Longton. If I don't get the official version of the story from you, I'll go to the gossip circuit for it.'

The lawyer revised his approach and eventually issued a statement. For a period of just under two years, his client Larry Stuart had conducted a close association with Mrs Denise Longton, who was for part of that time separated from her husband, Bernard Longton; for the last six months of the association, Denise Longton has been a divorcee.

Ray Bush asked if the lawyer would object to his client's fingerprints being taken, for purposes of elimination. The lawyer said yes, he would object – if necessary, in the strongest terms. His client had done nothing to merit being treated as a felon, nor had he attracted the attention of the police on suspicion strong enough to make a record of his fingerprints a legal necessity.

Ergo, no prints.

'Bernard Longton said the same, only more nicely,' Ray Bush said. 'He claimed he was big on civil liberties and even though he had no fear that his prints would ever incriminate him, he wasn't going to prejudice his freedom of choice just to help some technician do something the easy way.'

Without consent, the prints of Longton and Stuart could not be used, even if they were obtained by covert means. If either man were to be charged with a criminal offence, of course, then prints could be taken without their consent. So at that point there were two prints on record which matched nothing in the criminal data, and so far the police had no way of knowing who had made them.

The padded envelope was now being examined by a ballistics expert, who had decided, from marks on the inside of the packet, that it had contained a flat box, and, judging from the width and depth of the imprint of the box, probably five sticks of gelignite. There was no sign of a detonating device in the envelope, but something which was probably the firing mechanism had appeared among the debris collected during the grid search at the scene of the explosion.

Fragments of a small box had been found at various points outside the house; they were easy to pick out because of the particularly vivid green paint used to decorate it. At the laboratory the pieces were painstakingly collected together; there were 117 of them. A team of four people set about reconstructing the box. It took them two days, working long hours, but when they were finished it was possible for the ballistics expert to swab the inner surfaces of the box and find traces of gelignite.

'They found more than that,' Ray Bush said. 'Incredibly, and I mean incredibly, some child had scribbled inside the box with a crayon. It was faint and hardly visible at first, but in the right light you could see it, clear and unmistakable. *Tina* it said, in big, unsteady capitals. And guess what? Larry Stuart's second kid was called Tina.'

This time Ray Bush went directly to Larry Stuart's home.

The maid let him in and asked him to wait. Less than a minute later, Stuart came storming through the house, demanding to know why he was being harassed at home.

'I could have told him I wouldn't normally do that, which was true, but if I'd told him that, I would then have had to explain that the reason I did it with him was because his lawyer had tried to scare me off from doing any such thing, and I don't like parasites trying to intimidate me. But I didn't say anything about why, I just said I wanted him to confirm a piece of childish handwriting for me.'

From an envelope containing several pictures, Bush produced a close-up photograph of the writing from inside the box. Stuart frowned at it. He asked Bush what he wanted him to say. Bush said he should just say if he recognised it. Stuart said no, he didn't.

'You have a daughter called Tina?'

'There are millions of Tinas,' Stuart said. 'Probably a couple of thousand in Los Angeles alone.'

Bush asked if he could show the picture to Mrs Stuart. No, Stuart said angrily, he did not want her dragged into this. But Mrs Stuart was already there, standing across the hallway, a tall, attractive woman with steady intelligent eyes. She had been a senior technician with a Japanese electronics company before she married, Bush recalled, and he could not stop himself wondering what a woman like that, with her looks and talent, had seen in a stuffed-shirt like Stuart. She came forward, unsmiling, her face expressionless. She put out her hand to Bush.

'I'm Lilian Stuart,' she said. 'What do you want me to look at?'

A child appeared, a small girl, and came to stand beside Lilian. Bush handed over the picture. As Lilian studied it he took the other pictures from the envelope and immediately the little girl stabbed a finger at the colour print on top of the

143

bundle and said, 'There's Binda's pencil box!'

Bush looked inquiringly at Lilian Stuart. Binda, she explained, was how the youngest pronounced Belinda, the name of the eldest child. Bush now realised that Larry Stuart was gaping at his wife.

She handed back the print and asked if she could speak to Bush alone. He nodded and she led him into a small reception room off the hallway, leaving her husband and the child standing there.

'I assume you were about to unveil your findings a piece at a time, like in a thriller,' Lilian said as she closed the door. 'You'll forgive my impatience with that kind of thing. I sent that package to Denise Longton. I assume you already know that.'

Ray Bush did not want to disclose his ignorance, or injure his luck. He simply stared at the woman, hoping she would tell him the rest. Before she did she sat down, took a cigarette from a box on the table and lit it. 'I made the explosive device from industrial gelignite packed in an old pencil box,' she said. 'I would never have dreamed that the box would survive.'

Bush told her she should come to the station before she told him any more. She said she understood, and asked him to wait. She left the room, and when Bush went back out to the hall there was no sign of anyone. For one unreasoning, panicky moment he thought they had all run away. Then Lilian Stuart reappeared, wearing an outdoor jacket. Larry was at the door of another room, two of the children beside him, watching. Before leaving, Bush told Larry he would have to speak to him later.

At the station Lilian confessed to a long-burning hatred for Denise Longton that had culminated in her going to see the woman, taking with her a bundle of love letters Denise had written to Larry Stuart and which Lilian had found in his wall safe – 'I've been able to open it for years, he never realised . . .'

Lilian had brandished the letters and told Denise she knew all about her sordid association with her husband. She said Denise must consider the harm she was doing to a family. She demanded that the affair be ended. Denise said she didn't think she could do that. 'I told her that if she didn't break with Larry, those letters would blow up in her face one day. I suppose she believed I was speaking metaphorically.'

Bush recalled the tiny fragments of notepaper the document experts were still trying to reassemble.

'I really thought I would get away with it,' Lilian said. 'Then, on the other hand, I didn't care too much. I knew if I could lose Larry to a woman like that, I could lose him to any number of others. I still love him. It's just a terrible pity he doesn't seem even to like me, much.' She stared at Bush for a moment. 'I'll miss my children,' she said.

Later that day, it was confirmed that Lilian Stuart's fingerprints matched the two on the padded envelope. When she was told how much evidence had survived the blast, she confessed she was astonished. Technicians, she concluded, should not attempt serious crimes. They lack the imagination needed for the job.

Following an undefended prosecution for first-degree murder, Lilian Stuart was jailed for life. In prison she appeared to make a good adjustment and was allowed to work on special projects in the long-term prisoners' electronics workshop.

Two years after the verdict, she learned that Stuart, who had divorced her in the meantime, had married a dancer. Six months later Lilian's youngest daughter was killed by a hit-and-run driver who was never apprehended. That Christmas, after working for ten days on a personal project in the prison workshop, Lilian showed the finished article to the guard in charge of the workshop. It was small and cylindrical, no bigger than a handbag-sized aerosol.

'She told me it was a prototype portable blood-pressure monitor,' the guard later told a panel of inquiry. 'I don't understand these things, but I thought it looked very neat.'

Less than ten minutes after the guard had congratulated her on her work, Lilian applied the extending electrodes of her device to the sides of her neck and electrocuted herself.

Settled Accounts

René Blum, a forty-six-year-old Parisian, was the district police chief in a group of three small towns to the south of Mézière, in Ardennes, northern France. While Blum, a withdrawn and humourless individual, was not the most popular man in the region, it was generally acknowledged that he did his job well, and he was possibly the most dedicatedly honest man anyone in the district had ever met. Under Blum's cold, steady eye, the crime rate in his area of jurisdiction showed a steady decline during the first four years he was in the job.

In February 1979, to mark the fourth anniversary of his appointment, Blum's wife organised a family party at their home. They had no children, but six nephews and nieces were invited, together with their parents and Blum's mother and father.

'I worked hard to make the day special,' Mme Blum later told a friend. 'He never enjoyed parties, but I knew he took some pleasure in having his family close to him. I had even made arrangements for another officer to be called into the station – even if there was a grave emergency. Nothing was to spoil our day of celebration. Now that I've had time to think about it, I'm sure we can destroy happiness by anticipating it too strongly.'

147

Halfway through the extravagant luncheon, when everyone had eaten well and the specially hired staff were clearing the table to make way for more, René Blum was suddenly taken ill. He excused himself, stood up and took three steps from the table. Then he had to reach out to the wall to support himself. 'I think it is far too round to carry,' he said, mystifying everyone. 'The colour is wrong . . .'

He turned and glared at everyone for a moment, his eyes running along the faces at the table, then he began swaying and visibly turning pale. The next moment he collapsed. Two of his brothers carried him to the bedroom and laid him on the bed.

'I remember as his head went back on the pillow, he sighed,' said his youngest brother, 'but it wasn't the sighing sound a person makes when he lies down, it was all the air leaving his body. He was dead, I could see his eyes lose their sharpness. It was horrible, quite unbelievable, because a few minutes before, with the wine he had drunk and the wonderful food, he had become quite jolly, and that was unusual. Now this. Dead. We just couldn't understand it.'

Because Blum was a senior police officer, his sudden death had to be taken very seriously by the authorities.

'There were no suspicious circumstances,' one of his colleagues said, 'but you can never be sure, because so many people harbour grudges where a policeman is concerned, especially one as powerful and, frankly, as strict as René was.'

The body of René Blum was taken to Mézière, where an autopsy was performed by Georges Dufour, a state-appointed forensic pathologist.

'Upon opening the body, I found that the stomach and intestines were of a bluish, congested appearance,' Dufour said, 'and the intestines, particularly, looked engorged with blood. Upon examining the interior of the skull, I found that the meninges – the three membranes enclosing the brain and spinal cord – were hyperaemic, which is to say they contained an excessive quantity of blood. In view of the fact that the dead man had eaten a great deal of very rich food shortly before he died, I collected the entire contents of the stomach and had them sent for analysis.'

Dufour was reasonably sure that the signs indicated Blum had been poisoned, but he had no idea what poison might have been used. The laboratory results were not conclusive, either: they indicated the presence of something that did not match the nutritive qualities of the other material from Blum's stomach. A special analysis would be needed, from the Institut Analytique Nationale in Paris, and that would probably take ten days.

In the meantime René Blum's successor was appointed. He was Olivier Léger, a much more cheerful and dynamic man than Blum, who assured his staff that if it should prove true that his predecessor had been deliberately poisoned, then his first job would be to bring the poisoner to justice.

Three days after Léger took office, the mayor died suddenly, just after eating dinner. His sister, with whom he lived, reported that he had stared at her suddenly, muttered something about cold hands, then slumped forward, completely dead.

Dufour performed an autopsy on the mayor and found much the same internal appearance as he had noted in the bowels and brain of René Blum. 'Something else I noticed, too,' he said. 'Rigor mortis seemed to be diminished, its onset was slow and the usual full stiffness did not develop before the body became supple again. The same thing had happened with Blum, although I was not so aware of it the first time.'

Dufour mentioned this extra finding to a chemist at the laboratory in Paris, who thanked him and promised a result of the first analysis quite soon. The deceased mayor's stomach contents were bottled and sent to Paris for comparison with Blum's.

'This was not the best situation for a new police chief to walk into,' Olivier Léger admitted, 'although I had to remind myself that it was this situation, or the beginning of it, that was the reason I got the promotion in the first place.'

Detectives were appointed to check on the source of all the food used in the dinners which preceded both deaths. Nothing unusual was found – the produce was local, bought from local retailers or, in the case of certain vegetables, home-grown.

'I was drawing some comfort from the tidy lists that were accumulating,' Léger said, 'when the third death occurred. This time it was the headmaster of the local secondary school. Ten minutes after finishing his dinner, he had been standing in the garden, taking the evening air, when he stiffened suddenly, shouted something incomprehensible to his wife, then dropped dead.

'That made it an all-out murder hunt. Three prominent members in a local community did not die one right after the other in that way, not naturally, anyway. Our determination to find Blum's poisoner was swamped by a sudden drive from the Prefecture in Paris.'

Because it was Léger's district, he was still nominally in charge, but he found himself being 'assisted' by police officers with much more experience of murder investigation than he had. Dozens of officers descended on the area, interviewing people door-to-door, working fast to establish any and all links between members of the public and the men who had died.

The preparation of the report from the laboratory in Paris had been sharply accelerated. When the verdict on the first specimen landed on Dr Dufour's desk he said he had the feeling he had slipped back in time and was at the centre of a hunt for one of the classic murderers. 'Mushroom poisoning,' he explained. 'One of the oldest forms of assassination. Blum was found to have eaten *Agaricus campestris*, the edible mushroom, in fair quantity, but among these traces was a heavy presence of *Amanita phalloides*, a very poisonous strain.'

The headmaster had eaten poisonous mushrooms, too. Now that the laboratory knew what to look for, the results came back swiftly and botanists werc brought in to search the surrounding countryside to see whether the poisonous mushrooms were growing anywhere near the edible variety.

'They found none of the poisonous kind at all,' said Dufour, 'and while they were still looking there was an additional piece of information from the laboratory in Paris. They had discovered traces of the redcap mushroom, too, although in very small quantities. It was in the stomach contents of all three men. The redcap is an hallucinogenic fungus, pretty poisonous in its own right, but it was believed that in combination with *Amanita phalloides* an accelerating action took place, speeding the poisonous effect and in all probability intensifying it, too.'

After the botanists had gone, specialists in the rearing of mushrooms arrived, seeking out sites where the redcap and other exotic strains might be grown. Léger busied himself trying to establish a link between the three men who had died, while his deputy worked with a list of people in the region who might reasonably be expected to know how to concoct a sophisticated poison.

'The dead men, although linked by their civic prominence, were not notably conncctcd in any other way,' Léger said. 'It was known, indeed, that René Blum did not get on with the headmaster, and his relations with the mayor were cool. The mayor, for his part, was no friend of the headmaster – one was a Catholic, the other a Protestant – and the mayor simply avoided Blum whenever he could, because the two men did not see eye to eye on the local arrangements for car-parking. As for the headmaster, the poor man had always been too busy to be involved with anybody outside his working environment. So as far as I could determine, there had been no tangible link between the three men.'

The investigation began to drag. Nothing new was discovered, no connections between the deaths could be unearthed (beyond the obvious one that they had all been poisoned in the same way), and the source of the poisoning could not be located, let alone a single suspect for the murders.

'The first inkling of a real clue, a pointer in the right direction, came from the Paris Laboratory again,' said Léger. 'They had a forensic chemist there who had taken a degree in toxicology and for a time he had acted on a government poison advisory committee, compiling leaflets on the dangers of certain ordinary substances and contributing to a national antidote directory. He was a very astute man, and he believed he knew about this mixture of redcap and the other poisonous mushroom. It had been used, he believed, in very tiny quantities as a tonic by a religious sect in Belgium in the 1930s.'

The chemist sent Léger and Dr Dufour copies of an article which was written about the subject in a scientific journal in 1935. The Belgian sect, known as the Listeners (they believed thunder and powerful wind were God's means of commanding attention, and that if they listened to Him at times of storm they would gain special understanding), had used a number of dangerous substances to enhance their awareness of divine communications, including strychnine, arsenic and laudanum, an opium preparation. The experiments with mushrooms had resulted in the deaths of a number of the faithful, but it was believed that the particular mixture known as *Lumina vera* ('true light') was, if taken in the tiniest quantities, and only after fasting, a key to the 'divine pathway of understanding'.

'And the *Lumina vera* was the mixture that had been used to kill three of our citizens,' Léger said. 'On the strength of that, I could have told myself I was looking for an adherent of the Listeners who still possessed the recipe for the mushroom mixture, and who held a grudge against our police chief, our mayor and one of our headmasters. It was hard to believe, but somehow I felt I had been told something useful, and that was long overdue.'

Then there was a fourth poisoning, a woman this time. Edith Radiguet, a middle-aged area librarian, collapsed during dinner and, thanks to the rapid action of her sister, was rushed to hospital where a harrowing stomach wash-out saved her life. Nevertheless, Edith was seriously ill for several days, and it was a week before Léger could speak to her. He was anxious to know if she had any connection, however tenuous, with the three dead men.

'She couldn't think, poor dear, she was still so very ill,' Léger said. 'But after a while, thinking and moaning, shaking her head, she suddenly brightened. "We were all on the picnic committee," she said.'

On the face of it this was not promising, but Léger pursued the thread. The picnic committee arranged the annual children's picnic, a day-out event for approximately 360 children, which usually took place in an attractive valley twenty miles north of Mézière. The committee had to decide on transport, catering and entertainment. A large part of their work – which was conducted by telephone and memo, without the members ever meeting – was to award contracts for the various services needed.

'Now my policeman's nose began to itch,' Léger said. 'I got the notes of the picnic committee and studied them carefully. There were suggestions for the appointment of stewards on the coaches, lists of names of people who would be asked to help with distributing food, others who would erect tents in case of bad weather, and still others who would be charged with providing the entertainment. Apart from anything else, I was learning that the organisation of a children's picnic is not a particularly simple matter.'

Léger studied the list of people providing food. He was still new to the area and few of the names meant anything to him, but his deputy was able to describe all of the twelve people who featured. Nine were housewives, one was a hotel chef, one was a man who ran a sandwich bar, and one was a local priest who specialised in making dainty cakes.

'I put my deputy on to the job of interviewing these people with a view to spotting the homicidal maniac in their midst, and while he was pursuing that unlikely task, I had a look at the other lists. While we were doing that, the hot-shot policemen from Paris were charging around all over the place, pursuing lines of inquiry they obviously didn't want to share with me – although I have to say that they remained very friendly. I returned the friendliness, but I didn't tell them about our picnic lists. That seemed only fair.'

On the list of companies suggested for the provision of coaches to transport the children there were notes by Blum and the mayor, and underneath the notes the deceased headmaster and the librarian, Edith Radiguet, had confirmed their agreement. The notes concerned the previous year's trouble with the firm of Jules Fort. He had provided three coaches at very competitive rates, but one of them had been very sub-standard – in fact a seat had collapsed as the coach was cornering on the way back from the picnic, and a child had been injured, though only slightly. The committee had decided that at the forthcoming picnic, still some weeks away, the contract for coaches should go to another firm, even though Jules Fort had again put in the most competitive bid.

'It wasn't much,' Léger said, 'but it was the only sign of possible disharmony I could find, and to be frank, my original little buzz of excitement was beginning to dwindle the longer I sat there going through the lists of people organising a picnic. I mean, being objective, it did look very much like clutching at straws, didn't it?'

154

Another note came from the analytical laboratory in Paris: the forensic chemist who specialised in toxicology had run some very detailed tests on the samples from Léger's multiple murder victims, and also on the specimens taken from Edith Radiguet, and he had located traces of oxidised bronze. Whoever made the poison, the chemist believed, had used a bronze vessel to concoct the mixture.

Léger, meanwhile, went to the offices of Jules Fort in a neighbouring town and asked to speak to the chief executive. He was told that the company was owned and run by Anna Fort, the daughter of the original owner, Jules Fort. Jules had recently suffered a stroke and was now paralysed. Anna ran the company from her home, where she also looked after her father, who could no longer care for himself.

Anna Fort, a robust woman in her late thirties, greeted Léger brightly and offered him coffee. They sat down to talk in the morning room, where Jules Fort, strapped into a wheel-chair, sat in a corner staring out at the lawn and the trees. Anna explained that her father did not speak any more, but that she was sure he had found some inner contentment now, after the years of struggling to keep his company going. 'It is small now, just a few coaches, but it is enough to support us.'

Léger could scarcely bring himself to explain why he was there, but he did, and Anna said she quite understood because with something so serious to contend with, he must surely have to explore every avenue. 'We were sorry the picnic committee didn't want to use our coaches this year,' she said, 'but we quite understood. I made it clear to the mayor that we hoped we could be of service at some future time, and the matter rested there.'

Léger apologised for taking up her time, accepted another cup of coffee just to be sociable, then left. On the way home he decided to call in at the local general hospital, where Edith Radiguet was still a patient. He asked her if she could confirm that when the tender of Jules Fort's firm had been turned down the matter had passed off without any ill feeling.

'Just the opposite,' Edith said. 'Anna Fort stormed into the mayor's office and demanded to speak to him. She accused him of favouritism; she said he had probably arranged to sabotage the bus seat last year to give him an excuse to put her father through hell.'

The stroke suffered by Jules Fort had occurred three weeks after the last picnic and the incident in which the child had been hurt. Anna Fort, according to Edith Radiguet, had told the mayor that the stroke was his fault; her father's anguish and agonising over the incident had destroyed his health. She had then stormed out, according to the mayor's secretary, saying that the committee had not heard the last of the matter.

Before going back to Anna Fort to see what she might say in rebuttal, Léger looked into her background. He learned that she was a trained accountant who had failed to find work in recent years because she was considered a hazard in the workplace – she was epileptic, and subject to sudden *grand mal* seizures. For four years she had lived with her father, earning her living as a quality-control manager in a small specialist foodstuff manufacturer's. She still worked at that job part-time.

Léger suddenly had no doubts left. He had found his poisoner. The possible connection between Anna working for a foodstuff manufacturer and people being selectively poisoned was not clear, but he still felt he had enough to justify pressure tactics. He told Anna bluntly that she had lied to him about her reaction to the coach tender being turned down. She took a moment to absorb his change of tone. Then her own changed. She told Léger he was another of them, the self-appointed and self-serving elite who ran everything according to a code that took no account of merit.

Léger said her speech became so rapid and so violent that he was afraid she might have one of her seizures. 'She ended up threatening me with lawyers, government investigators, all kinds of terrible fates, if I didn't get myself out of her house straight away. Of course I went – I had no option.'

Before he left, however, he did take note of one or two things. Having casually angled himself so that he could see into the back garden, where old Jules Fort was sitting at the side of the apple orchard, he found that he was staring straight into the kitchen, which he had imagined would be at the other side of the house. Léger had only a moment to take in what he saw, but he was sure there was a small, high-sided bronze pot standing on the floor by the cooker; he also saw a cellar trapdoor propped halfway up. On the way out he passed a picture of a woman with staring eyes, who looked as if she might be suffering from a thyroid complaint. The small brass plate at the bottom of the frame said 'Adèle Jouve, 1932'.

'Back when I was still a blundering young policeman,' Léger said, 'I was told by a much older officer that whenever I was anywhere that made me suspicious, I should memorise as many as possible of the things I saw then take away a headful for examination later. I had learned that that was very useful. I had also learned, with time, that small coincidences litter the annals of successfully solved crimes. But those two important lessons collided later that day.'

When he got back to his office, the forensic chemist from Paris was there. He had been attending a conference near-by and thought he would make a small detour and look in on the people with the fascinating poisoning case. Léger confided that he had a suspect, and that he hoped he would find a way of clearing the obstructions and making an arrest as soon as possible.

'The problem at the moment, I told the chemist, was that I had no proof, nothing at all I could use to link Anna Fort to the poisonings. While I was talking the name of the strange woman in the picture came into my head and I asked, "Have you ever heard of a woman called Adèle Jouve?" '

The chemist nodded without hesitation. Léger stared at him. Adèle Jouve, the chemist said, was a founder of the Listeners, the sect which devised the lethal mushroom tonic. The chemist had read all about her at one time, and had learned that she was something of a primitive biochemist, with a natural talent for creating herbal medicines. 'But she was also mad,' he said.

That evening the two men had dinner at a local restaurant and Léger told the chemist everything he knew about the case and about the woman he was sure – *really* sure now – was the villain.

'Why don't you just accuse her, right to her face?'

Léger pointed out it was easy for a forensic chemist to say that; there was more to solving a crime than just accusing your main suspect.

'But she is irascible,' the chemist said. 'She has no control over her temper, and she is clearly murderous. Such people cannot withstand the tension of anything delayed, they need it to be over and done with. I would bet you that if you let her think you have a great deal on her and that it's only a matter of time until you bring her in, then she will cut across the waiting and admit everything.'

Léger did not believe that, not entirely. As a proposition it had a certain appeal, however, and although there was the danger that he would only make his suspect dig herself deeper into her defences, he thought he might just try what the chemist suggested.

The following day he went to see Anna Fort, and as soon as she opened the door to him he hit her with his suspicions. He knew she had an interest in cultivating mushrooms he said – was that not true? His suspicion was based on nothing more than the sight of a cellar trapdoor and the connecting thought that mushrooms are often grown in cellars. To his genuine surprise, Anna became flustered. What if she did dabble with mushrooms, she demanded, what did that prove?

She had backed into the hallway and Léger followed her in. He pointed at the picture of the woman with staring eyes. 'Who's she?' he asked.

'My great-aunt,' Anna replied, surprising him again.

'A great-aunt who devised mushroom concoctions of the kind used recently to kill three people in this locality and to nearly kill a fourth.'

Léger believed that after that he was operating on automatic pilot. He just kept on talking. Instead of creating a tension with his pseudo-certainties, as the chemist had suggested, he appeared to have caused a collapse from the sheer weight of his onslaught. Anna was crying, one hand over her mouth, the other thrust out defensively in front of her. Léger heard himself mention the bronze pot, and all at once she was screaming at him and punching at his arms and telling him to stop.

'I got a police officer to come in and keep an eye on her father and we went to the station. Anna, calmer now, told me quietly where the mushrooms were grown, where the tissue was for growing more, and, most important of all – because I hadn't had a clue – she told me how she poisoned her victims.'

No one had been prepared for the answer. Anna had used an accomplice. He was Max Fargue, the oldest of the drivers who worked for the firm, a man deeply loyal to Jules. Like her great-aunt before her, Anna had converted him to a cause. This cause was a vicious brand of revenge, but Anna convinced Max it was his fight as much as hers.

'She just waited around for opportunities,' Léger said. 'In the case of the mayor and Edith Radiguet, she had Max create a diversion at the front door while she waited at the rear of the house, ready to slip into the kitchen.

'Anna did careful research, largely by simple snooping, and

159

when she was sure she knew the dinnertime drill at the mayor's house, she got into the kitchen while the sister dealt with Max at the front door. Timing was vital – the call at the front door had to happen when the food was on the plates, or was partly on the plates, so that she could add the mushroom paste to the correct dinner portion. With Edith Radiguet it was especially easy – she lived alone and all Anna had to do was get into the kitchen, add the paste to the cooking pot, and leave.'

There had almost been a tragic complication on the night Anna chose to poison Edith Radiguet, because of Edith's sister's visit. But the sister called just after she had begun her meal and did not eat herself, so the poisoned food wasn't shared. And if the sister had not shown up, Edith would almost certainly have died.

In the case of René Blum's party, what might have appeared to be a very difficult time to attempt a selective poisoning turned out to be the easiest. Blum's wife had called at the shop attached to the food manufacturer's where Anna worked. She bought several items for the celebration meal, then asked the woman who managed the shop if she could recommend any staff to serve at table for a one-off occasion who would not cost her a fortune. The manager told Mme Blum she would see who she could muster. The first person she approached for help was Anna, who offered the services of Max Fargue, saying he was not only cheap but a trained waiter, too. Technically, the first killing was carried out by her accomplice, but, as Anna rationalised it, all the real work was done by her.

'And, rather quicker than she had planned, Anna had accomplished her first killing. The books, as she put it to a psychiatrist, were beginning to look straight. Above all, she liked to see accounts properly settled. When Blum died, she could hardly wait to get the rest of the picnic committee and settle all four of the accounts.'

The case never went to trial. Anna Fort was found to be

unfit to plead on the grounds that her mind was unstable and, in the opinion of three psychiatrists, swiftly degenerating. Olivier Léger believed she was sane but lethally vicious – 'Although that is not a diagnosis which is accepted in law, as yet.'

In the public interest Anna was committed to an institution for the criminally insane. Her accomplice, Max Fargue, was jailed for life.

Broken Heart

Cynthia Coogan was the daughter of a millionaire and the granddaughter of a millionaire. She had married one, too. At the age of thirty-eight she had more money than she knew about, and the entirely free run of homes in New York, Cape Cod, Seattle and Washington. Once a year she flew to Europe, where she spent a month shopping around the fashionable capitals and entertaining old and new acquaintances at her apartment in Florence. Robert Coogan, Cynthia's husband, never travelled abroad with her, but each summer they spent six weeks together at their Cape Cod retreat.

In the early evening of Monday 9 October 1973, Robert Coogan called the police from his home at Sutton Place, New York, and reported that his wife had been murdered. In less than ten minutes, detectives, a photographer and two laboratory technicians were at the scene. Coogan led them to the spacious sitting room where his wife sat at the end of the chesterfield, one hand dangling over the back, the other lying open, palm up on the lap of her mustard-coloured wool skirt. But for one incongruous feature, Cynthia Coogan might have been sitting there waiting to receive guests, her brown hair immaculately in place, her make-up flawless. The incongruity was a stout kitchen knife sticking out of her chest on the left side. Beside her on the couch was a pool of dried blood.

In his statement to the police, Robert Coogan said he had come home at five-thirty as he usually did on a Monday, and as usual he let himself into the apartment with his key because on Monday their maid, Annie, had the day off. 'I put down my briefcase in the hall, walked in here and there she was, just sitting there. I thought at first she was staring at something on the wall, you know, the way she kept on staring over that way and not turning when I walked in and spoke to her. Then I saw that knife.'

He said he had stood in front of his wife for maybe five minutes, stunned, unable to touch her, or to run to the telephone, or to act on any of the other impulses that struck him one by one and moved away, leaving him numb. 'I simply couldn't take it in. It was like I had side-stepped into an alternative world, someplace not real that I wasn't supposed to know about . . .'

When pictures had been taken, the body was removed to the morgue and the technicians began working their way through the apartment, dusting for fingerprints and using filtered vacuum-cleaners to collect specimens of fibres and hairs from the carpet and furnishings. Robert Coogan went to the station with the detectives so that his fingerprints could be taken for elimination from the dozens that would be picked up in the apartment. While he was at the station he also made a more detailed statement for the record.

'Cynthia came back from Europe two weeks ago,' he told Detective Steve Lambert. 'She had spent four weeks away, basing herself in our apartment in Florence and visiting various places – Rome, Paris, London. She saw lots of friends while she was in Europe. Since she came back she had been calling round, meeting New York acquaintances, getting ready for the autumn season.' He smiled wryly at the detective. 'Cynthia lived for the social scene. I have nothing against it,

I suppose, but the work ethic attracts me much more.'

In his report, Detective Lambert described Mr Coogan as a handsome, well-groomed man in his early forties, a former Ivy Leaguer who had taken control of his family's banking and insurance companies in the mid-sixties and had acquired a reputation, according to back issues of *Fortune* magazine, for 'benign aggression in the take-over market and in the growing business of pension-fund management, for which he displays an instinct forged from hard work and enthusiasm.'

'I had never been close to the tycoon type before,' Detective Lambert said. 'It's true what they say, the rich *are* different, especially that kind – he had been born rich and had gone on to get even richer by his own efforts. He knew all about power: it was instinctive with him, I suppose. I kept feeling I should do things for him while he was in the office, he had that kind of effect on me, like he was a natural boss, definitely king class, and I was definitely a born servant, or a peasant who had got lucky enough to rise to the level of servant.'

Coogan took the death of his wife in a stoical fashion which Lambert assumed to be the result of breeding: he wouldn't do anything so vulgar as to break down and cry, or get angry, or get so choked up he couldn't speak.

'I asked him to think of all the people he knew that his wife knew who might even remotely harbour a grudge, or be angry about something that had happened recently, mad enough to put a knife in her ribs. There were no signs of a struggle – the apartment hadn't been disturbed – so we were assuming, for the time being anyway, that whoever killed Cynthia Coogan had been let into the apartment without any kind of resistance. Coogan put his hands over his face when I told him it would help to have a list of least-favourite people who were still part of the couple's social circle. He said it would be hard, maybe impossible, since he believed his wife had known a lot more people than he had, but he would do what he could and let me have a list as soon as he could.'

The autopsy on Cynthia Coogan was performed by Dr Hector Ortega, an Hispanic American who had trained as a forensic pathologist in Los Angeles and was therefore, by his own description, devoid of belief in human redemption. Mankind's destiny, in Hector's cheerfully voiced opinion, is to blow away like so much tumbleweed and leave no worthwhile mark on the earth. 'What people do to each other,' he said, 'rats wouldn't do to each other. Snakes wouldn't, not even cockroaches. Man is a ghastly mistake, a blunder of cosmic wiring, and when he's gone and lets the animals have the planet back, it'll be a nicer place.'

Hector's autopsy reports (in America they are called protocols) are curiously at odds with his smilingly cynical outlook. He is a profoundly good pathologist and will follow a line of suspicion, however slight, by any possible means until his suspicion is confirmed or in some other way resolved.

In the report on Cynthia Coogan he wrote that the body was of a well-nourished Caucasian female, mid to late thirties. There were no visible outward deformities or disfigurements, and the only distinguishing marks on her body were a tiny mole on her abdomen an inch below the navel, and a two-inch scar on the back of her left leg below the knee. Following a note about Cynthia's weight and height, and the observation that she had engaged in sexual intercourse a short time prior to her death, he went on to describe the way she appeared to have died.

A kitchen knife, weighing 50 grams (1.75 ounces) overall, with a carbon steel blade 10 centimetres (approx 4 inches) long, was forced into the chest at the left fourth intercostal space, to a depth of 5.4 centimetres (2.25 inches), at a distance of 84 centimetres (3.25 inches) from the left

166

margin of the sternum. The point of the knife penetrated the right ventricle of the heart, causing copious bleeding into the pericardial sac.

Cynthia had died from internal haemorrhage, Hector concluded, at some time during the twenty-four hours before the body was brought to the morgue. At the end of the report, Hector inserted an extra forensic observation:

Close to the place where the tip of the knife came to rest, and on the blade itself, there are traces of a substance which superficially resembles sand, or very fine gravel. Some grains of this material are visible on the surface wound, and would appear to have been carried to the interior of the body by the sheer force with which the knife was thrust through the wall of the chest.

Within twenty-four hours Robert Coogan had produced a list – three typed pages – of people who might conceivably have had sufficient dislike for his wife that they might be driven to attack her.

'It's taking small things to the extreme, of course,' he told Detective Lambert. 'I can't really imagine any of them doing it, but there are a few people on there who have certainly let it be known that they do not think much of my wife or myself. The worst of them, the ones who have shown their dislike publicly on more than one occasion, I've put a star against.'

Asked whether he had had sexual intercourse with his wife on the day she died, Coogan hesitated, then said yes, he had: they had made love an hour before he got out of bed on the morning of Monday 8 October.

The murder of Cynthia Coogan was a sizeable media event, but Robert Coogan's policy of silence and a loyal refusal to speak on the part of those closest to him meant that the story soon dwindled to the centre pages. After four days it disappeared completely as the police worked their way, with no success at all, through the list of possible murderers Coogan had given them.

On Saturday 15 October, a young woman called Deena Shawn called at the police station and asked to speak to the detectives investigating the murder of Mrs Coogan. She was eventually seen by Steve Lambert, who noted that she was clearly very worried.

'You can tell when the worry is real, and runs deep,' he said. 'They forget to be nervous. The station makes any newcomer jumpy, but this girl had the bug-eyed-fright look you see on some girls that are just naturally nervous. Except when she spoke to me she was deadly earnest, very concerned, and she didn't take her eyes off mine once while she talked.'

Deena's room-mate, Annie, had gone missing. Annie was the maid at the Coogans' house, and according to Deena she loved the job and would never have walked out of it, as other people were now assuming she had done. Annie was supposed to have come back to their shared apartment in Queens on the evening of Sunday 7 October, but she never showed. When after a couple of days she still hadn't appeared, Deena rang the Coogans' number, even though Annie had asked her never to do that except in the direst emergency, and she spoke to a new maid, who said Annie had left, and she had no idea where she had gone.

It was only that afternoon that Deena found out that Mrs Coogan had been murdered. The news startled her, and she wondered if there was any connection between the murder and her room-mate's disappearance, but she couldn't think what it would be, and didn't want to think about the possibility anyway. After some constructive thinking, Deena began to wonder if Annie had gone to visit her only relative, a brother in Michigan, but when she called he said he hadn't seen his sister or heard from her in months. By Friday Deena was deeply worried, and by Saturday she was worried enough to walk into the police station and put her half-formed fears to the detectives.

'She thought Annie might be rolled up in the murder in some way,' Lambert said. 'And who could blame her for thinking that? Her friend goes missing, for the first time in her recorded history, the day before her boss gets murdered. Two big events, both centring on people who were connected – *ergo*, there's a link. And there was, of course – though it wasn't one little Deena managed to think of.'

Detective Lambert took details of Annie from Deena, plus a photograph of the two of them together, and promised that the police would do all they could to trace her. The next day, Sunday, Lambert called at Robert Coogan's fine house in Sutton Place. He apologised profusely for intruding. Coogan did not seem perturbed.

'I told him I was concerned about the fact that his maid appeared to be missing, and he hadn't told me about it,' Lambert said. 'He looked like I'd handed him a puzzle. He couldn't see what the problem was. "Maids go missing all the time," he said. "Lord knows how many we've had through this place. They come, they go, and half the time when they go, they take something valuable with them." That much made Annie different, he said – she hadn't taken anything. What with the disruption in his life, it was halfway through Tuesday before he realised she was gone, so he called the agency and hired another maid.'

Lambert filed the report, sent a copy to Missing Persons, and promised them he would send along anything else that turned up on the girl. The assumption was, as it always is with women over eighteen in New York, that if she wanted to disappear, and she hadn't committed a crime, then she could disappear and not reappear until she was ready. Vanishing in

New York, for a non-felon, is remarkably easy.

On the Sunday afternoon Lambert had a call from a private detective who wondered if he might make an appointment on a reasonably urgent matter. 'That tickled me,' Lambert said. 'PIs, they always come on like they're the most hesitant, most law-abiding people you ever came across, and they're so mannerly, it's just a pain to listen to them. For the most part they're lower than shit, of course, but when this one said he had something that might be linked to the Coogan case I thought I'd better accommodate him. I told him I'd meet him in a diner near Broadway, because I didn't want him coming into the station. Contamination's not a thing that usually troubles me, but I have to draw the line somewhere, right? I'm just very leery about letting PIs walk into the police station and sit down on the furniture.'

At the meeting the private detective revealed himself to be as sleazy as Lambert had expected, but he appeared to be a fastidious operator, which was unusual. He produced papers to show that he had been hired by a Mrs Dorothea Lewis to keep a tail on her husband, Charles Lewis, a diamond importer with a retail outlet on Fifth Avenue where he sold cut stones and a limited line of finished jewellery.

'The detective said that this Lewis was very big-time, the biggest-timer he'd ever had to tail. The jewellery he was selling was one-off pieces, made up just for the kick of it, the prestige, because no matter how exotic or how expensive the stuff was, he could always sell it. His wife told the PI that she knew her old man got to meet some very smooth ladies in his line of business, and she suspected that he was currently seeing one. She had got to a point – probably fraudulently but what the hell – where she was financially independent, independent enough anyway to divorce Lewis, and if she could get a nice fat settlement at the same time, fair enough. So she wanted the PI to get the dirt on Charles Lewis as fast as he could.'

The private detective had a flair for theatre, Lambert said, because just when the story did not seem in any way to concern the Coogan investigation, he produced photographs taken on a beach at a secluded spot near Cape Cod. They had been taken on Thursday 4 October, using a camera fitted with a 300mm lens and mounted on a stabilising clamp in the private detective's car. The pictures clearly showed Charles Lewis walking along the smooth, polished-looking expanse of sand, his arm around the shoulder of Cynthia Coogan.

'Until he saw a photograph in a three-day-old newspaper,' Lambert said, 'he hadn't known that the woman Lewis was seeing was the murdered socialite. So far, he had not shown the pictures to anyone, not even Lewis's wife, because he had wanted to get some more to justify the rather high expenses he would be claiming. Now he felt, rightly, that the game was suddenly too rich for his blood and he was handing it all over to the police. I thanked him and went back to the station with everything he had on the Lewis case.'

According to a map provided by the private investigator, the location of the beach where the pictures had been taken was only two miles from the Coogans' Cape Cod house. Lambert noted that for the record, but decided in the meantime that he should say nothing to Robert Coogan about this development. Late that evening, Lambert called at the morgue to identify the body of a liquor-store owner killed in a hold-up – the store was on the corner of the street where Lambert lived and he used it often. While he was there he saw Hector Ortega hurrying about the place, his green shirt, apron and trousers heavily stained with blood. Lambert wanted to talk to the pathologist but thought the next day might be better, when he was less busy. However, when Hector saw Lambert he waved and invited him to join him on his coffee break.

They sat in the small office with coffee and doughnuts and Lambert told Hector about the PI turning up with the picture of Cynthia Coogan, taken only a short time before she died. Hector frowned and cocked his head at Lambert.

'The sand then, eh?'

It was a moment before Lambert realised what he was talking about. 'Then it hit me. The sand. I hadn't even given it a thought. Time and again you get that on the autopsy notes, some person or other turns up dead with a knife in them, and some junk or other has got forced into the wound by the impact of the stabbing. It's common and you tend to overlook it after a while. Now Hector was all wide-eyed and enthusiastic-looking. "I kept a sample," he said, "just a few grains, as much as I could scrape on to a microscope slide." '

Hector got the specimen, which had been clipped to the file of duplicate records. On an impulse he also went to the freezers and ran a small suction collector over Cynthia's hair. A few more grains of sand appeared. Hector brought it all to Lambert and asked him if he would organise something else at the same time as he was having the sandy material assessed.

' "Check Mr Coogan's blood group," he said. I asked him why, and he said it was just perfectionism on his part – he hated anything to be left hanging in the air, which was his way of saying he doesn't like to be in the dark about one damned thing.'

The sample on the microscope slide, plus a specimen bag with the few grains collected from Cynthia's hair, was sent to one of the world's few forensic palaeontologists who worked, at that time, in the Smithsonian Institution in Washington DC. Lambert attached a brief note, asking the expert to compare the sample with another which would reach him in a few days; in the meantime, could he put together an opinion on the composition, structure and origin of the sample? That kind of evaluation, Lambert explained, is always impressive when presented to a jury.

Lambert next sent a telex to the police in the area of Cape

Cod where Cynthia Coogan and Charles Lewis had been photographed together. He asked them to send him a specimen of the sand from the beach depicted in a picture accompanying his telex message.

'Then something truly terrible happened,' Lambert said. 'It was the kind of thing that cuts across all the hardening you get in this job and touches your shrunk-up pity. A body with ropes on it showed up in a pile of garbage in the yard at a public incinerator. The body was pretty badly broken up, the arms and legs all floppy and smashed, the skull flattened, but it was recognisable. It was Annie, the Coogans' maid.'

Hector Ortega examined the body at the morgue and concluded that after the young woman had been tied up with two lengths of rope around her arms and around her calves, she had been laid on a road and a car had been run over her at least three times.

'When we hosed off the blood and the garbage,' Hector told Lambert on the telephone, 'we found some excellent tyre marks. I'll send you up pictures.'

The sand sample arrived by express messenger from Cape Cod and Lambert forwarded it to the forensic palaeontologist. Minutes later, he was called to a telephone on one of the radio lines: it was the police at Cape Cod. He went into the radio-phone room prepared to acknowledge the receipt of the sand and thank everyone concerned, but the officer he spoke to didn't want to talk about sand. He thought it important, in view of the interest New York Homicide was taking in a particular quarter of Cape Cod, to tell Lambert direct that the body of a New Yorker, Charles Lewis, had been washed up that afternoon. The body was badly damaged and it looked as if it had been in the water for some time, but there was identifying information sewn into Mr Lewis's shirt. Furthermore, as a dealer in raw diamonds he needed to carry such ID, and his laminated fingerprint card had definitely tallied with prints taken from the body.

'I sat back and thought about it for a while,' Lambert said. 'My real instinct was to run all over the place yelling about the way things were turning out, but I'd done that before and made myself look a jerk, so I decided to cogitate. While I was doing that I had a call from Hector Ortega, asking me if I'd got the word on Robert Coogan's blood group. I had forgotten about it. I got a clerk in homicide to handle it straight away. He got the information from the passport office, and then confirmed it with the vehicle licence people.

' "The group is O," I told Hector. He laughed, the crackly sound he makes that passes for laughing. Then he told me that Cynthia Coogan had sexual congress with a man shortly before she died, but it wasn't her husband. The gentleman who pronged her was group AB. And that was official, Hector said, because he'd had the semen tested in our own lab.'

By the time the sand samples had been confirmed as identical, Lambert decided it was time to visit Robert Coogan. He took with him one other detective as a witness, and one to do a little specific snooping.

Because Lambert was now sure that Coogan had killed not only his wife, but Charles Lewis and Annie, too, he did not even try to be impartial in his approach to the interview. He told Coogan that the knife in Cynthia's chest had furnished an identification. 'And when I said that, I saw the flash in his eyes – I saw it because I was watching for it. Only a split-second, then he shut it off, but he knew for sure there were no prints on the knife, even though we hadn't told him so.'

Lambert explained that the knife had picked up some traces of local debris which clearly identified the spot where she died. 'And it wasn't here, Mr Coogan. She died at Cape Cod.'

Timing was now crucial: Lambert believed Coogan was overbalanced by this sudden spotlighting of himself, and would not be able to muster anything in the way of a convincing defence.

'Did she die before or after you ran over Lewis and dumped him in the sea?'

Both detectives watched as Robert Coogan went through a variety of expressions, as if he were trying to find one that would sit still on his face. Finally he stood up, ran both hands through his hair, then sat down again. His studied calm and his air of detachment both seemed to leave him at the same time. He looked from one man to the other, clearly on the verge of tears.

'I had a broken heart,' he said. 'Not much of a defence, but I know it's enough to make you murderous. It's either that or despair.'

He told the detectives how he had known his wife was 'up to something' when he called her during the last week of her stay in Florence and she had already left, several days before; she had told the woman who looked after the apartment that she wanted to go home early. Coogan was a powerfully connected man and it did not take him long to find out where his wife had gone. 'Anyway, I already knew about the diamond merchant,' he told Lambert. 'I kept telling myself it was nonsense, but that was a hard piece of self-deception to sustain, since my suspicions are never nonsense.'

He had driven to Cape Cod and confronted the pair of them in the kitchen of Lewis's rented beach cottage. Lewis had behaved despicably, saying that Cynthia had led him on. Coogan listened for as long as he could, then lost his temper and hit Lewis. They began to fight and Coogan hit Lewis over the head with a steel poker. 'It killed him, I think. But I took him out on the road and ran over his body a couple of times. It's what the Japanese used to do to their victims when they were nearly dead. They believed the smashing of so many bones at one time could reach down even to the levels near death and inflict an extra dose of pain.'

Since Coogan and Lewis had begun fighting, Cynthia had been locked in a bedroom, refusing to come out. Before leaving the cottage with Lewis's body, Robert Coogan made sure she could not escape by ramming a candle into the keyhole. He took the body out to sea in Lewis's launch, dumped it and came back. He then had a drink in the kitchen, thinking about what he should do, listening to his wife moaning in the bedroom. In the end he decided he could never forgive her. The thought of her adultery would tear him apart. So he decided to kill her, too. He took a kitchen knife from a drawer and kicked open the bedroom door. As it swung inward Cynthia rushed past him, out of the house and down the beach.

'I chased after her and I soon caught up. Without hesitating at all I swung her round and shoved the knife into her. She yelped, just a tiny sound, then she fell down. I caught her, carried her back to the cottage, and cleaned us both up.'

He burned the outer clothes Cynthia had been wearing and dressed her body in clean clothes from drawers in the bedroom. At that point he had known her disappearance would cause a flurry of media activity, so he thought it best to stage a murder.

'I confess, if I'd been more calm, less torn inside, I would have staged it differently.'

'But you would still have killed her?'

'Oh yes, both of them.'

He even remembered to bring back blood-soaked towels in a plastic bag to create the pool on the couch. Bringing the body into the house had been no problem, either, since one thing guaranteed by a dwelling in Sutton Place is a private, high-walled rear garden.

'The only real problem was Annie,' Coogan said. 'She stayed here on the Sunday night, instead of going home as she was supposed to do. I shuffled straight into her, dragging the body. She stared at me for a second, then she went crazy. Screaming, waving her arms. I grabbed her, hit her, ran after her when she broke away and hit her again. Oh, it was a mess, a nightmare, really. I made sure she was dead – ran her over, like Lewis, because I hated her at that point, hated knowing she would have reported me if she had been able . . .'

When Coogan was putting on his overcoat, preparing to go back to the station with the detectives, he asked if the clever pathologist who had found the sand on the knife had noticed that the knife had been pulled out of the wound, then put back again later. 'It was the only way I could get her clothes off and on,' he said.

Lambert said he was pretty sure Dr Ortega hadn't noticed that. He looked at Coogan and detected a glimmer of a smile. Killing Cynthia had certainly assuaged something in him, Lambert decided. Perhaps it had even cured his broken heart.

As the three men left the house the third detective came forward. He held up an envelope and shook it.

'More sand,' Lambert told Coogan. 'From the underside of your car.'

'Just in case?' Coogan asked.

'That's right,' Lambert told him.

A Life Apart

Occasionally there are mysteries where no amount of police investigation or scientific analysis will yield an answer, and yet everyone involved feels that the answer is there, just beyond their reach, waiting to be discovered. The case of Simon Grant was just such a case.

In a letter addressed to the director of social services in Rifton, Sussex, a military historian called Maxwell Grant wrote, 'It was never our intention, when we separated, that the boy should suffer, but at the same time we had to respect his wish for independence. The dilemma was especially acute with Simon being disabled, but in the end he proved his willingness and ability to look after himself, so we bought him the little house and left him to conduct his own life.'

Simon Grant had suffered a birth injury which paralysed the left side of his body. He could not use his left leg, which had to be supported with a brace, but the arm, although stiff, was mobile and he had the use of the hand. Wasted neck muscle meant that his skull was relatively unsupported on the left side; when he was tired his head tended to hang over that way. He had grown accustomed to this, as to all his other infirmities, and seemed unaware of how his shuffling gait and sometimes lolling head made people wary of him on first sight.

179

'His face didn't help, either,' a police officer said. 'He always had his mouth hanging open, and he wore these spectacles with great big thick lenses that made his eyes enormous. He was clean enough, but his hair was never washed for some reason, and it was hardly ever cut, so it stuck up in clumps all over his head. What with the way he moved, and the head hanging over to one side, and that face – it really did startle people the first few times they saw him. Add to that the fact he was short-tempered and never seemed friendly to anybody, and you had an unpleasantly unique member of the community.'

Simon's mother and father had separated when he was eighteen, and he had made it clear that he did not want to live with either of them. He had even written out his reasons for wishing to be left alone: he wrote of wanting a life apart, without interference from other people. He had a private income from a fund set up by his grandfather and he lived on that, spending his days studying obscure books about Eastern religions and learned (but outdated) papers on medicine.

'I wrote to his father around the time Simon was twenty,' the director of social services at Rifton said, 'because I was concerned about someone with Simon's disabilities living alone. I wanted some kind of reassurance that he was all right, and that the father knew exactly his son's circumstances.'

It has been said that the social services were snooping, since Simon gave no outward signs of distress or hardship, and he never asked for anyone's help. He lived alone in a three-bedroomed bungalow on a quiet road and ventured out only twice a week to do essential shopping. A police officer remarked that, had he been physically normal, nobody would have paid the slightest attention to him.

Simon was twenty-two when he went to spend a short holiday with his mother in Devon. It was early in the summer of 1987. His mother had told friends that it was time she played

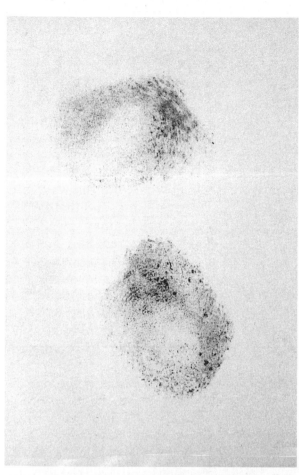

Love Letters: Chemical disclosure of Lilian Stuart's fingerprints on the bag in which the bomb was delivered to Denise Longton.

Fragments of letters from the blast, tiny but perfectly legible.

Settled Accounts: *Amanita phalloides*, the highly poisonous mushroom also known as the Destroying Angel, the main ingredient in the concoction Anna Fort used to kill three people.

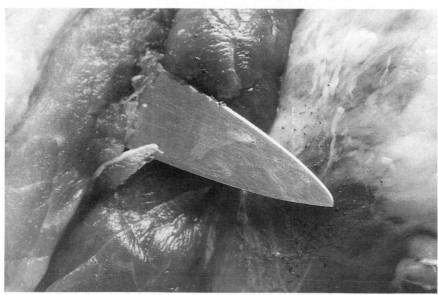

Broken Heart: Interior of the knife wound which killed Cynthia Coogan, with visible grains of Cape Cod sand.

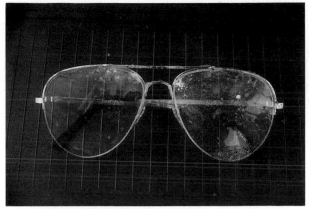

A Life Apart: Maxwell Grant's spectacles, recovered from the ground. Some of the material adhering to the frame was human brain tissue.

Incubus: Print developed on the barrel of the gun Jeff Adams was careless enough to strike with his finger.

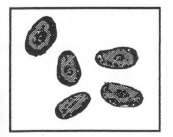

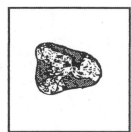

There is broad variety in the sectional characteristics of human as well as animal hairs, depending on site of growth. Top – head hair; lower left – pubic hair; lower right – a single moustache hair.

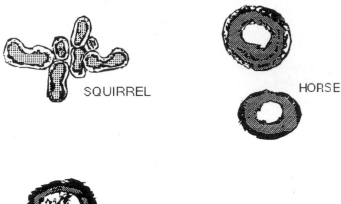

Superficially, similar animal hairs look widely different when they are viewed in magnified section.

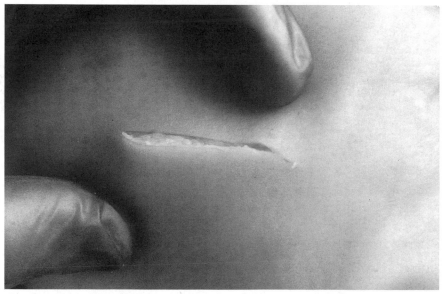

Conflict: Bloodless knife wound on a woman who was stabbed after she died.

more of a part in the boy's life, though her friends believed she was simply feeling guilty for having ignored the 'little troll' – as she tended to call him when she was drunk – for such a long time.

'He was certainly an odd one,' a neighbour of his mother's said. 'Polly Grant had never made any bones about the fact that she had a peculiar son, but he was a lot stranger than we had bargained for.'

He arrived in a taxi on the Monday, the neighbour said, and he and his mother went out into town a couple of times during the first two days of his visit. After that he did not go out. 'And neither did his mother. That was most peculiar, because Polly was one of those women who wanted to be out at the shops all the time. It was a big part of her social life – mingling in the town, seeing acquaintances, stopping for chats with them and going for cups of coffee. She used to go out every day, but less than a week after her son arrived, she stopped going out altogether. I never saw her again.'

Nobody ever saw Polly Grant again.

'After the first week had passed, and still there was no sign of her, I began really watching the house in earnest,' the neighbour said. 'At night I saw a light go on in the living room, and occasionally I would see the son's head in profile as he sat watching television, or reading by the fireside. At about midnight the light would go out, another would come on at the side, where the little guest bedroom is, then a few minutes after that the place would go into darkness.'

Ten days after Simon had arrived, the neighbour went across and knocked on Polly Grant's front door. Her concern had taken a sharp upward turn when she recalled that it must be over a week now since Polly Grant had had a drink, and that had to be a record. Polly never kept a reserve of alcohol in the house, because she knew she would simply keep drinking it until it was gone, so she went out and bought supplies every day.

The neighbour had to knock several times before the door was opened. Simon stood there in his shirtsleeves, head lolling, mouth agape. 'I introduced myself and asked him if I could speak to his mother. He said she had gone away for a while. Oh, I said, I didn't know she was planning a trip. To London, he said; she had gone to London to see a friend, and he had agreed to mind the house for her. Before I could ask him any more he mumbled something about the gas and shut the door on me.'

The neighbour did not know what to do. She went on watching the house, then, two days after she had spoken to Simon, she spoke to the police. They took a statement and promised they would look into the matter. But before they got around to calling at the house, Simon left. The neighbour saw him being helped into a taxi in the early evening. She called the police again and told them what had happened. They sent round a patrol, and one of the officers made a careful survey of the house from the outside, shining a torch through the windows and searching the two small outbuildings.

'Not a sign of anyone,' a police officer said later. 'We did think, at the time, that the neighbour was probably making too much of her friend's disappearance, but nevertheless we checked thoroughly. All we could say was, there was no sign of another person, alive or dead, at the house.'

Neighbours of Simon's in Rifton saw him return from his holiday, as unkempt and shambling as before. In his absence there had been a complaint about a smell emanating from somewhere in his back garden, but a tentative survey by council employees had revealed nothing, and by the time he came back the smell had gone.

Back in Devon, when a month had elapsed and there was still no sign of Polly Grant, the neighbour called the police again and reported her as a missing person. The police found this rather melodramatic, but they reviewed the matter and decided there were grounds for an investigation. A magistrate's warrant was obtained to open the locked-up house, and three constables and a sniffer dog went in.

'They found nothing,' a police officer said, 'but it wasn't exactly an ordinary uneventful search. The dog went mad for a time, running from room to room, barking, sniffing in corners. He wouldn't settle and eventually he had to be taken outside because his erratic behaviour was just getting in the way. The house was thoroughly searched but there was nothing at all to suggest anything was out of order. Mail had piled up behind the front door, but there was nothing significant there, either. We put through a call to Rifton Constabulary, explained the position to them, and asked if they wouldn't mind going round and asking Simon Grant just where exactly he thought his mother had gone.'

The first thing the Rifton Police noticed was the terrible smell in Simon's house. A PC and a WPC were reluctantly shown into the living room, which their report described as squalid. There was half-eaten food on several plates on the table, mouldy meat on a tea tray on the sideboard, and the floor, chairs, and sofas were littered with empty and half-empty crisp packets.

'The smell on the air,' said the policewoman, 'was like sewage. It was in every room and I just couldn't understand how anybody could live in there, with all the windows shut, breathing anything so foul. I began to feel sick after five minutes and I had to go outside.'

While she was catching her breath in the back garden, the WPC saw numerous half-rusted chemical containers and large empty bottles lying about in the dense, uncut grass. In a three-sided outhouse she found a four-foot high steel tank filled with thickish brown liquid that smelled like soup.

'On the matter of his mother's disappearance, Simon was not at all cooperative,' the constable said. 'He told us she had gone to London and asked him to look after the house for her. He had done that for a while, but when she still hadn't come home or telephoned to tell him what was going on, he decided to come back to Rifton.

'All the time he was telling me this in his droning voice, his head hanging over like something out of Frankenstein, I kept wondering just what this was I'd walked into – it was really bizarre, that filthy house, the stink, this really weird young man at the centre of it all. When I was sure he wasn't going to tell me anything useful, I asked if I could take a look around, and before he said anything I got out into the hall and did a swift survey of the other rooms. It was completely out of order to do that, but I acted on an impulse that told me I'd stumble on something terrible, something that would justify me nosing round the house without any right.'

He found nothing illegal or especially bizarre, apart from a box lying just inside one of the unfurnished rooms: when he peered inside he saw that it contained three dead kittens.

'I asked him what happened to them and he said he thought somebody had poisoned them. They'd been born in his garden, the mother cat had got run over by a car and he had decided to rear the kittens on his own. The previous day he had gone out to feed them at the back where he kept them and they were all dead in the box, just as I saw them. I suggested he buried them and he said yes, he would do that later in the day.'

Before the police left, the WPC asked Simon what was in the tank at the bottom of the garden. Simon said it was a solvent he was working on. She asked what kind, and he told her sharply that she wouldn't understand.

Rifton Constabulary told Devon Police what Simon had said about his mother's absence, and the small file was set aside. It was not closed, however, because a detective at Rifton had become interested in what the two visiting officers had reported. The detective was John Foster, a DI with twenty-two years' experience.

'From what I had read, I could identify Simon Grant as a seriously unbalanced type,' he said, 'although it hardly needed an experienced detective to spot that. There was nothing I could do right then to gain any further knowledge of the man, but I decided to stay alert to anything of interest that might emanate from that direction.'

Simon's father arrived from his home in Portugal on a visit in the spring of 1988. He visited the local pub on the day he arrived and spoke to a few of Simon's neighbours there. He said the state of the place frankly worried him, and he did not believe his son was quite as capable of tending to himself as he had previously insisted. 'Arrangements may have to be made to have him come and live with me in Portugal,' Maxwell Grant said, loudly enough for a number of people to hear him. 'Things really can't go on as they are.'

And that evening was the last time anyone saw Maxwell Grant. On the day he arrived he had put an expensive pair of boots into a repair shop to be mended. The repair had been expensive too, because Maxwell had insisted that real leather be used, and that it match the quality of hide from which the boots were made. When ten days passed and he hadn't called to collect them, the cobbler rang the local telephone number Maxwell had left to tell him that the boots were ready for collection. The man who answered the telephone said Mr Grant had gone back to Portugal several days before. When the cobbler demanded to know who was going to pay for this expensive job he had just done, the man on the phone said he couldn't help him.

A few hours later, DI John Foster was told he might like to speak to a woman who was waiting in an interview room. She had come to register her concern for the safety of Maxwell

Grant. The woman was Delia Moran, the wife of the landlord at the pub where Maxwell had had a few drinks on the day he arrived in Rifton. She told Foster that she was sure something bad had happened to the visitor.

'She said he had promised to go back to the pub the following day, but he never showed up,' Foster said. 'That wasn't a worrying thing in itself, but after ten or eleven days, when she realised that none of the other customers had seen Maxwell Grant since that first day, Delia Moran asked around the town. She learned that the cobbler had been expecting to see him; so had the local travel agent, who was arranging a return flight, and the bookshop had bought in a couple of reference books he'd ordered to take back to Portugal with him. Like the cobbler, Delia Moran had called the house, and Simon had told her the same story – his father had gone back to Portugal.'

The travel agent had not been approached again about the ticket for Maxwell Grant's return flight. John Foster made a call to the Portuguese police in the town of Portimão, where Maxwell Grant lived, and asked if they would check whether he had recently returned from Britain. Within the hour, the Portuguese police were back on the line: Mr Grant's house-keeper, they had learned, was very concerned that she had not heard from him in two weeks, not since he left to visit his son in England.

'It was time to visit Simon,' Foster said. 'Nothing I had already learned had prepared me for the state that house was in. It was foul. He was a hoarder of old magazines, newspapers and empty polystyrene containers, and when I saw that, it strengthened my conviction that he was disturbed. That kind of hoarding of useless rubbish is a symptom of certain kinds of mental disturbance. I didn't need that to convince me he was dippy, though. The man himself was one big loose-tied bundle of peculiarities – Christ, he really was odd. He walked with the aid of a stick, and he leaned so heavily on it you would swear he was going to slip, and his head hung over. None of that would have mattered, I'm sure, if it hadn't been for the total impact of that head – the way he looked at you through the pebble specs, and the fright-wig hair, and the hanging-open mouth with its yellow teeth and the tongue that looked like it had been boiled. He was only a young man, but the air of dereliction and the sense of breakdown and decay was abominable. To finish the effect he had a smell like rancid butter.'

Simon was not pleased to see DI Foster, and he made that clear. He listened to questions about his father, then acted as if he had heard nothing. Foster found himself trying to get tuned in to a special wavelength, Simon's hearing mode, but he decided after a few minutes that Simon was putting on a show.

'I told him we needed to know more about his father, and if I didn't leave there with a satisfactory answer about his whereabouts, a search team would come out to the house and pull it apart until some trace of the man was found. Simon straightened up his head at that, pushed the specs up on his nose and told me I was harassing him. I assured him he didn't know what harassment was, but he soon would do if he kept on treating me like a berk.'

Simon became more communicative from that point, but he would say only that the day after his father's arrival, he decided he had to go back to Portugal. 'He didn't say why,' he told John Foster. 'He just left.'

'Did he go in a taxi?'

'Yes.'

Foster made a credit-card call from Simon's telephone to the local taxi firm. Their record showed no pick-up from that address, although they did have a record of taking a passenger there just over a couple of weeks earlier.

'It was some number he had in a notebook,' Simon said

when he was challenged about the taxi. 'I've never seen the driver before, or the car.'

Foster told Simon bluntly that it was a bit of a dark coincidence that first his mother did an overnight disappearing act, and now his father. 'I think we're going to need that search team over here,' he said. 'Is there anything at all you want to tell me before I call them?'

Simon looked away. Staring at the window, he said, 'I'm going to file a complaint about you. This is harassment.'

An eight-man team came and worked their way through the house from front to back. They checked everything, including the drains and the tank of soupy liquid at the bottom of the garden. They found some disgustingly mouldy food, a number of old medical books which had been partly hollowed out and colonised by mice, and a number of cat skins. But there was no sign of Maxwell Grant, or of any of his possessions. Foster admitted that he had imagined the search team would find the suitcase tucked away under some sacks somewhere, then perhaps the clothing at the bottom of a compost bin. But there was nothing.

'The only mysterious thing they found, apart from that tank with its sludgy, soupy solvent or whatever it might be, was a thing that looked a bit like a dagger with a curved handle topped off with a steel ball. It was lying at the bottom of the tank, and the liquid appeared to have made it shine.'

The object was photographed and copies were faxed around the stations, in case anybody might know what it was. In the meantime Foster got on to Devon Police and told them what had been happening in Rifton. On the strength of what Foster said, they decided they would conduct a proper search of Polly Grant's house.

They found nothing particularly suspicious, but two dogs they took into the house behaved strangely, becoming very agitated, just as the dog had done at Polly's house. In spite of finding nothing, they decided that something bad had befallen Polly Grant: her neighbour told the police that Polly had several times bemoaned the fact that, because she had hammer toes on her right foot, she could hardly ever find shoes that were comfortable, and she therefore cherished the few pairs she could wear. 'Five pair of shoes in total, she had,' the neighbour told the police. 'Five and only five, I could describe them all to you.'

She did describe them, and the police discovered, ominously, that all five pairs were in the house. Polly's one and only pair of slippers was there, too. With the help of the neighbour, the police were able to discover that almost certainly, all of Polly's clothes were in the house, too.

A positive identification came back on the odd steel object found in the sludge tank in Simon's garden. It was the femur section of a hip replacement joint. Another call was put through to the Portuguese police: could they find out if Maxwell Grant had had a hip replacement operation? The answer came back less than two hours later: Mr Grant's doctor in Portimão reported that in 1986, at a hospital in Maida Vale, England, Mr Grant had had a successful operation for the replacement of his left hip joint, which had been severely arthritic.

A full forensic team was sent to Simon Grant's house. They took away tools from the shed, the complete contents of the tank in the garden, and over a hundred incidental items that might display marks or traces which could possibly be of use in determining what had happened to Maxwell Grant.

'The hospital in Maida Vale sent us the numbers and other particulars of the replacement joint that had been fitted into Grant,' Foster said, 'and sure enough, that was the one we had found. The feeling, far-fetched though it might be, was that Simon had somehow managed to dissolve his father in that tank down in the garden. The lab chemists had analysed the stuff, or they had tried, and it turned out to be a real pig of a mystery. As far as they could tell, Simon had mixed together a lot of different acids, and then some alkalis that would have neutralised the acids, and then he had added other stuff – panain, for instance, which digests protein. He wouldn't say what he had put in there, but his earlier claim, that it was a solvent, was now taken seriously by several people. The only trouble was, our lab technicians couldn't really dissolve anything in it.'

The gardens were dug up at Simon's house and at his mother's; drains and sewers were searched with miniature television cameras and swabs were taken of the linings of pipes, grilles and drain covers. Substances that might have been blood were collected, as was material a technician found on a saw blade and thought looked like bone marrow. Everything from microscopic examination to DNA profiling was tried on the samples, but they all came up negative. There were no organic traces of Maxwell Grant to be found, and no significant remains of his former wife.

'It was creepy, because we didn't even find a fingerprint of Maxwell Grant's at the Rifton house – think of it, we had part of his hip joint, but no dabs,' said Foster. 'Throughout all the back-and-forward searching and sifting, the constant traffic of police and forensic personnel, Simon just sat about the place, reading old books or newspapers, or staring into space. He looked for all the world like he was in another dimension and was aware of none of the commotion that was going on around him.'

Sixteen days after the investigations at the houses in Rifton and Devon began, it was decided that even in the absence of bodies, it would now be safe to charge Simon Grant with the murder of his father. Nobody seriously doubted that his mother was dead too, but without any indication that she had come to harm, it would have been difficult to make an adequate prosecution case.

'Another officer and I went round to Simon's house to charge him and bring him in,' John Foster said. 'We found Simon dead in a chair at the table. His head was lying sideways in a puddle of vomit.'

A post-mortem examination showed that Simon had died of arsenic poisoning. No arsenic was found in the house or in his pockets. The only traces of the poison were in his system.

'He left nothing to tell us what had happened,' Foster said, 'and no clues were found when a forensic team, from London this time, did a second sweep of both Simon's house and his mother's.'

The case never reached the preparation stage for court, and the record was finally filed away. A final enigmatic touch was the discovery, eight months after Simon died, of adult cat skeletons buried under a tree at the side of the house. Among the bones was a pair of gold-rimmed spectacles, wrapped in greaseproof paper, later identified as the spectacles Maxwell Grant had worn at the time he arrived in Rifton.

'The forensic people did score one winning point, which is more than can be said for the police,' Foster said. 'They soaked off a dry, flaky material that was stuck here and there to the legs and earpieces and nose bridge of the glasses, and they subjected it to several kinds of very careful analysis. In the end, they were able to say that it was definitely human brain tissue.

'The discovery didn't do anything to help solve the mystery, but it certainly made it more intriguing.'

Best Wishes

In a letter to his brother Harry in 1965, Thomas Kemp wrote, 'I am determined that by the time I am fifty, I will have my life organised just as I want it. Two years to go and you'll agree things are not quite ideal, but just you watch, my best wishes from now on are reserved for myself, and I'm going to see they're fulfilled.'

Thomas had just come out of prison after a three-year stretch for passing forged cheques from a stolen chequebook. At the time of his release he possessed exactly £1 10s in cash, the clothes he wore, plus a spare shirt, spare socks and underwear. He also had a travel warrant that would get him from Birmingham, where he had been in jail, to Blackpool, where his mother had agreed that he could stay with her until he had found a job and could afford to rent a place of his own.

'Thomas had had an extraordinarily chequered career,' said his probation officer at the time, Doris Yuille. 'He was a trained service engineer for a firm manufacturing lifts. It was a good job and he had been good at it, but stability made him edgy – he was restless almost from the time he completed the qualification period. That was when he was twenty-two. From that time onward he went through a succession of jobs, everything from a porter in a meat market and an assistant to a signwriter, to deputy floor manager – complete with forged credentials – in a television studio and a salesman of luxury cars in Mayfair. He never stayed in any one job for more than a year, because he was chronically unable to stick to an enthusiasm for long, and when he wasn't enthusiastic about something, he didn't want to know about it. It was all or nothing with him, total commitment or none, in every aspect of his life.'

In prison Thomas had attracted the interest of the warden, who believed there was something of the unshaped genius about him. He encouraged him to express himself through writing and painting, particularly the latter, for which he showed a flair.

'I learned afterwards, though,' the warden confided, 'that Kemp was an inverted kind of prodigy, the kind that can only work against the grain. Show him a system, and his instinct will be to find a way of overthrowing it to his own advantage. That was another thing – he really abused everybody and everything he feasibly could. What you had, in short, was an attractive personality fronting a thoroughly negative, self-serving waster.'

Thomas's first job on arriving in Blackpool was to convince his mother that he was a changed man. With his record that might have been hard to do, but his mother had an abiding tenderness for her younger son. She believed him when he told her he was sick of living on the edge of life and that he wanted to be a part of society, he wanted to contribute and earn himself a place.

'With his mother convinced of his good intentions,' Doris Yuille said, 'the pressure was no longer on him to find a place of his own to live. As long as he was trying to make something of himself, his mother would be supportive. And, God bless her, she was. She was a widow living on a small income from an investment made by her husband, a Co-op shop manager.

After a year of living with her, and paying no rent or any part of the food bill, Thomas was actually accepting half of the weekly allowance that his mother drew from the Co-op bank.'

On the pretence of seeking work, Thomas was spending most of his time in bookmakers' shops, placing daily bets on the races in the hope of hitting a big winner. When he wasn't in a betting shop he could be found in a pub, reading the small ads in newspapers and magazines, trying, as he once said in the hearing of an off-duty policeman, 'to see a crack I can wriggle through'.

Doris Yuille said that she was aware there were murky developments in Thomas Kemp's life around that time, but she could never pin him down to a clear explanation of how his time was spent, or find out from other people what he might be doing. 'He was being given job interviews, but nobody was keen on hiring him. It was much later that we learned he would confide to prospective employers that he had a skin allergy that was susceptible to whatever it was the company manufactured or distributed; if it was an office job he would say he was epileptic. In every case he apologised, saying he was obliged to attend the job interview, unsuitable though he was, because otherwise his unemployment benefit would be cut off. So he was sure of his weekly benefit, plus the nice supplement he picked up from his mother, and about fourteen months after his arrival in Blackpool he was into the porno business as well.'

Among Thomas's acquaintances in the pubs along the front at Blackpool were a number of young prostitutes, and with two of them, plus a young freelance photographer in need of work, Thomas revived the pornographic postcard trade. He spent no money of his own on the venture, apart from a few pounds for advertising in seedy magazines; the girls and the photographer were to be paid their percentage out of the proceeds. Notebooks which surfaced years later suggested that Thomas kept 80 per cent of the profit from the pictures. The real surprise was that he sold so many; 230 sets of postcards at £3 a set were sold in the three-month period before Thomas lost interest and abandoned the project.

'He knew that if he ever got caught doing anything dishonest again, he would end up back in jail, and for quite a long stretch next time,' Doris Yuille said. 'But he really did give the impression that he was doing the upright thing and was trying to build a decent life for himself. I must say, I believed all that.'

Eight months before his fiftieth birthday, Thomas Kemp turned from a con-man and petty thief into a violent criminal. He was later to become a murderer, too. Forensic psychiatrists who later tried to evaluate his case could not understand the change in him, which amounted to a personality swing. The transformation did not mean he lost his cunning, however; when he first turned to serious crime his name never appeared on any list of suspects.

The first act of violence was planned calmly, as if he had been that kind of criminal all along. He knew that every morning the landlord of a particular pub went to the bank at 10.30 with the previous day's takings. The ritual was no secret – the landlord was a big man and perfectly capable of defending himself from an attacker, or even two. The weakness in his manoeuvre was that, after years of going to the bank at the same time every morning, Monday to Friday, without ever being impeded, he had grown complacent.

Thomas Kemp waited until a Monday morning, when the green money bag would contain all the cash taken in the pub over the weekend. For five minutes before the landlord walked along his usual route, Thomas had been standing there, twenty yards from the door of the bank, dressed as a clown, his face completely anonymous behind the make-up as he handed out leaflets (snatched the previous week from a supermarket) to passersby.

As the landlord drew near Thomas dropped the leaflets into

a waste bin and pulled a plastic squeeze bottle from his pocket. The landlord scarcely looked at the clown as he greeted him cheerily, waving one hand in the air as the other came up in line with his eyes and squirted a jet of ammonia into them. The landlord dropped to the ground, clutching his eyes. Thomas knew that no one could have noticed any violence – they would simply be confused by the sight of the man on the ground. So without hurrying, he bent down, picked up the money bag and pushed past a couple who had come forward to look. They recalled later that the clown had said he would get the police.

There was £600 in the bag, which in 1967 was a considerable amount of money. Thomas used almost £100 of it to buy himself new clothes, and thereafter he did his reading and drinking in the bars of expensive hotels rather than in the seafront pubs. He continued to sign on for unemployment benefit, and still accepted half of his mother's weekly allowance.

'He was entirely amoral,' a psychiatrist later declared. 'He cared nothing for the feelings of other people, and it may have been an extension of that indifference that made it possible for him to turn to violence, although it is rarely ever that straightforward. You might think that a man at his age would have become rather fixed in his behavioural framework, and in general you would be entitled to think that. But Thomas Kemp gave every sign of going through some kind of delayed adolescence, with sudden changes of tempo and rapid shifts in his underlying moods. To everyone who encountered him at that time he seemed like a rather charming, very calm individual, but in fact he was largely out of control.'

According to his own view of things, Thomas was at that time as far outside the mainstream of civilised society as he could get, and he wanted to stay there. To do that he needed to have no worries about money, and having found how easy it was to commit a robbery with just a little planning, he decided

197

to try a few more. By doing that, by making just a small effort in the meantime, he could guarantee his long-term security and his freedom to do just what he wanted.

The second crime of violence involved the use of a fake firearm, which did not daunt Thomas at all. He bought a plastic assembly kit and put together an automatic pistol that looked real enough. His disguise this time was to be glasses and a wig – he had seen big-time entertainers visiting Blackpool use the same cover, and he had been amazed at how it could alter a comedian's or singer's appearance to the point where he was unrecognisable.

On the appointed day he travelled by bus to the near-by town of Lytham St Anne's so that he could be reasonably sure he would be dealing with strangers. The shop he had selected was one he had watched from the street several times. It was an off-licence with a door situated directly opposite the counter, so that both entrance and exit could be made in a fast straight line. The daily trade was good and, as far as Thomas knew, the large till was only emptied at closing-time.

Wearing a grey wig and heavy horn-rimmed spectacle frames, he waited outside until there were no customers in the shop, then he strode in, brandishing the fake gun. The woman behind the counter took a moment to register what was happening before she saw the gun. Then she put both hands to her breast and for a second Thomas thought she was having a heart attack. He yelled at her to empty the till into the carrier bag he was holding. The woman froze for a moment, but when he shouted at her, repeating the instruction, she punched open the till and dragged out the notes between the fingers of both hands, throwing them into the open mouth of the bag. It took no more than ten seconds, and when she began trying to scrape the coins out of their trays, Thomas dropped the gun into the bag on top of the money, took out his squeeze bottle and squirted ammonia in the woman's face.

As she went down behind the counter, howling and gasping, Thomas twisted the carrier bag shut and marched out of the shop. On the pavement he made a sharp turn left, then another, getting himself into the alley alongside the shop. Behind a parked van he took off the wig and glasses, put them in the bag with the money and the gun, and put that bag inside another one of a different colour.

Then he sauntered out on to the street, stopping to look into the off-licence. He saw the woman being helped by one man while another dialled the telephone on the wall behind the counter. Thomas waited until the police and ambulance arrived, then he walked along to the bus stop and caught a bus back to Blackpool.

'That hold-up netted him another £400,' the psychiatrist said, 'but far from making him feel secure, the neatness and success of the robbery had provided him with the kind of gratification that criminals are often keen to repeat. Almost at once, he was determined he would commit another robbery, once he had worked out the details.'

But the plan was side-tracked. Thomas had a letter from his brother Harry, saying he was coming to Blackpool to visit his mother and adding that he hoped he would see Thomas at the same time. The letter made it clear that Harry believed Thomas only used their mother's address as a place where his mail could be sent; Thomas had told his brother that would be the arrangement until he had a 'decent' address that he could put on his notepaper.

'Thomas was in a quandary,' the psychiatrist said. 'Here was something that did mean something to him. Most amoralists have one person in their lives whose views and feelings they care about. With Thomas it was his elder brother, a man with his own small business and a way of life that Thomas had never dared try to invade, because it was sacred territory. Now the revered brother was going to find out that Thomas still lived with his mother and still hadn't found a job. Oddly, Thomas would not spend money to get himself somewhere to live, not even in that situation, with the brother coming, and being well enough able to afford a place. Instead, he determined he would come up with some promise he could make to his brother, one that he could keep.'

Thomas's reverence was not reciprocated. Harry despised him and never missed an opportunity to tell him so. On the day he arrived in Blackpool, Harry's main priority, after seeing his mother, was to ensure that his brother was in gainful employment, staying out of trouble, and putting no pressure on their elderly parent. In the circumstances, Harry was not pleased. Thomas told him things were not as bad as they seemed. He did have a job, representing a firm which sold television advertising space. He had built up a nice little nest-egg in the bank, but he wanted to 'consolidate' before he started spending out on a place to live and all the other expenses which inevitably followed.

Harry was not impressed. He told Thomas that although their mother was in good health, it was not fair to keep expecting her to cook and to fetch and carry for him. She had been used to her independence before he got out of prison and she was entitled to have it back. Thomas promised he would move out soon. He was aware that his mother had not mentioned that she gave him money every week, and he was glad of that, but his mother *had* told Harry something which completely revised Thomas's view of his future.

'Almost in passing,' said the psychiatrist, 'Harry had said that they could not wish for a better mother and he was keen to see that her generosity and affection were never abused. "Lord knows, we do little enough for her," he had said, "and yet she's made sure we'll be comfortable when she's gone." Thomas was intrigued, of course. Without pressing too hard, and almost by making it seem that he knew the facts already, he wormed out of his brother the information that their mother had benefited to the tune of £30,000 when their father had died, the bulk of it their father's own wisely banked inheritance from his own father. The money was even now collecting interest, to be shared between Thomas and Harry when their mother died. Thomas had known nothing about that. He was stunned.'

The following week, Thomas got himself a flat quite near to where his mother lived. He furnished it neatly, had a telephone installed and did everything he had promised Harry he would do. He then entrenched himself in his new lair and thought very hard about what he must do next.

'That was the predator in him showing itself, the way he actually moved out of the old lady's house,' said the psychiatrist. 'He was putting himself at a distance he could strike from, and then withdraw. He couldn't do that under her roof. Apart from any practical considerations, it would have jarred psychologically with the kind of creature he was.

'Until then, he had been able to ignore his mother. She was somebody about the place who meant less than nothing to him. She provided shelter and food and money, but as a person she was nowhere. Now, suddenly, she was somebody, a target, so he had to be somewhere else, a place where his target could not know his movements.'

After a week of brooding, hardly going out and talking to no one when he did, Thomas decided to try to get in touch with a man he had met in prison, an old army doctor who had been struck off during the 50s. When Thomas met the doctor he was in prison for passing himself off as a retired colonel, spending several days and nights at top-class hotels, then leaving without paying the bill. He was caught because he tried the trick once too often and far too close to the previous place. In the recreation breaks in prison he had talked to Thomas about how a man of his appearance could easily pass himself off as a physician, and the talk had inevitably turned to the dark side of medical practice.

'This old man had told Thomas something about drugs that he thought might be useful in his present quandary, but he couldn't remember the details,' said the psychiatrist. 'So he made a real effort, calling the prison and pretending to be with the BMA, getting them to pass on the doctor's resettlement address and even the telephone number at that address.'

Thomas travelled to London and spoke to the doctor, who scarcely remembered him. The old man was an alcoholic, so Thomas did what any predator would in the circumstances: he took him out, filled him with drink, and picked his brains.

Two weeks later, Thomas telephoned Harry to tell him that their mother had been taken ill the day before. It had been nothing too serious, he added, but the doctor had said she must take things very easy – it was her heart. Harry went to Blackpool the following day. He found his mother looking shaken and pale, her eyes weary and perhaps a little frightened. He told her not to worry, then he went to see her doctor. She was fine, the doctor assured him: she had merely suffered a flutter, as many people of her age did; it was her heart's way of reminding her it needed more rest now that she was older. With care, the doctor added, she should have a minimum of trouble from the condition.

Thomas promised Harry he would look in regularly on their mother, and would do her shopping and take care of anything else she needed. He repeated the doctor's reassurance; she would be all right.

But two months later the old woman had another attack, more serious this time, and Harry was at her bedside within twelve hours. Again the doctor tried to reassure him, but this time he did say that some old people's hearts withstood the fluttering better than others; it was perhaps marginally unfortunate that his mother seemed to be susceptible to the debilitating side-effects that occasionally strike.

The third attack came within five weeks. This time the old woman looked very sick and frightened. Harry could not console her, and the doctor admitted it didn't look good. That number of attacks in that space of time, he said, plus the fact that the spaces between attacks were diminishing, could only indicate a rapid weakening of the heart. The doctor would do all he could, however, so Harry was to try not to worry too much.

It was a week to the day when Thomas called, at two in the morning, to tell Harry that their mother was dead. A suitably red-eyed, visibly grief-stricken Thomas met Harry and his wife at the airport as they arrived for the funeral.

The psychiatrist said: 'Thomas could remember that his brother's first words were, "This is a terrible day," and his own silent response, behind his sorrowing front, was, "Maybe it is for you, but it's the greatest day of my life!" Within two weeks he was handed a cheque for £15,000, his share of the inheritance. As he had told his brother nearly two years before, his own best wishes were for himself, and now he was in the state of comfort and security he had so confidently predicted.'

What happened after that was another puzzle for those trying to untangle the mystery of Thomas Kemp. Four days after receiving his inheritance he walked into a Manchester betting shop wearing a rubber mask and holding his imitation pistol. He demanded that the cashier handed over the money from the till. A customer hit him behind the ear with a lemonade bottle, and when Thomas's head cleared, he was being dragged to his feet by two police constables.

'He knew he was probably going to spend a terribly long stretch inside,' the psychiatrist said, 'and I think the fear of being discovered made him confess to the other robberies, just in case the police sprang a new arrest on him the minute he got out of jail.'

Thomas offered no explanation for why he tried to rob the betting shop when he had just banked such a comfortably large inheritance. Two forensic psychiatrists believed he had no idea why he did it. They tentatively suggested that he might have suddenly found it necessary to be caught, to be punished, but that was only guesswork. Nobody knew.

'And then, a day before he was due to go into court on two charges of aggravated robbery and a charge of attempted robbery, he asked to see the prosecution lawyer, and told him he had murdered his mother.'

Showing no trace of emotion, Thomas explained how he had asked his old prison mate, the struck-off army doctor, to explain how best a man could dispose of an elderly relative without raising a suspicion of foul play. The method, he was told, was to create a false heart condition, one which would apparently get worse and worse. The family doctor would establish a record of heart trouble. When the patient finally died, after the third or fourth attack, there would be no question of a post-mortem, because the doctor would be satisfied he knew the cause of death. A death certificate would be granted without question.

'He used digitalis, supplied by the old ex-medico,' said the forensic pathologist who performed a post-mortem on the exhumed body of Thomas Kemp's mother, shortly after he confessed. 'He administered it, I gather, in cups of tea he made when he went to call on her. The digitalis did no more than make the heart misbehave briefly, but of course in a woman her age, or even a younger one, the signs would most often be taken to signify a heart attack. And as he strengthened the doses and narrowed the intervals between them, her apparent heart condition got worse. Then he was free to kill her in any way and at any time he liked. In the event he used cyanide, a small capsule sold to him by the old medico. He gave it to his mother with a glass of water, telling her it was from the family doctor, a little something for her heart.'

The irony, the pathologist said, was that the old woman's heart was in very good shape. Without interference, she would have lived on for a good number of years.

Thomas would probably have lived a long time, too, without his own interference. In a note he left, he explained that while he talked to the ex-doctor about the best way to kill his mother, he also received – and paid for – advice on how to carry a lethal dose of poison around with him, so that it could be used at any time. He bought two cyanide capsules and was taught the technique of carrying the second one in a rubber bag in his anus.

After lengthy evaluations of his mental state, following which the psychiatrists declared him sane, Thomas was tried and sentenced to imprisonment for life. He cut the sentence to three days and died with his face pressed against the window bars in the prison library.

Incubus

Los Angeles is one of the leading manufacturing, commercial, financial and international trade centres of the United States, and of course it is the centre of the US motion-picture industry. Not surprisingly, it also has one of the highest crime rates for a American city – 'and the most colourful one, for sure,' said Richard Housey, a physician and criminologist, the author of an influential study of the LA crime scene, *Designer Crime*. Housey has lived in the Garden Grove area of Southern LA for twenty-five years, and in that time he has been involved in the investigation and recording of thousands of crimes. He has often done duty as deputy coroner and supplementary police physician during periods when the law enforcement agencies have been under pressure.

'This beautiful place has the unfortunate side-effect of attracting lizards,' Housey said. 'Charles Manson was one, but there have been many others who have attracted less publicity, even though some of them were much worse than Manson – certainly more imaginative.'

Housey described a series of murders in 1988 which became known as the 'San Gabriel Ghoul' killings. 'That was what they were called in the papers, and inevitably the public caught on to that name. But to the police and others closely connected with the crimes, this was the Incubus case.'

Incubus was the name signed on a series of notes, twelve in all, sent over a three-week period to Sally Wimbush, who shared a villa with her husband and her mother at San Gabriel, to the north-west of Los Angeles.

'Sally was a very striking young woman, even by local standards,' said Housey. 'Until the time of her marriage to Jim Wimbush, who was a studio accountant, she had been a fashion model working exclusively for one of the larger fashion houses in these parts. Her face and figure were on every advertisement for their top-of-the-range lines and she appeared in every upmarket glossy, including *Vogue* and *Harpers*. She gave it all up at the age of twenty-six, though, when she met and married Wimbush. It was rumoured that he'd laid down certain pre-nuptial stipulations, and her retirement from the public gaze was one of them.'

Sally Wimbush did not live long to enjoy her retirement. On a warm, moonlit night in late August 1988, she was raped and murdered by the swimming pool at her home. Her body was found in the morning by her maid, who told Housey that after she got over the horror of the event, the thing that kept playing on her mind was that she could never have imagined such a loss of dignity in the elegant Sally.

'Sally had been stripped,' Housey said, 'and laid on her back on a marble bench by the pool, then her hands and feet had been tied to the legs of the bench. She was sexually assaulted, then every external orifice of her body had something stuck in it. A bottle was rammed into her vagina, a ballpoint pen in her anus, her mouth was packed with dog excrement, and wooden chopsticks were driven through her eardrums. She was left to die of suffocation and God only knows what level of pain.'

The police knew about the notes Sally had been receiving – she had called the local station after the second one arrived. The detectives had done what they could: they ran handwriting and other forensic tests on the notes, had copies circulated to psychiatrists and psychotherapists, to probation officers, social workers and a number of care professionals, on the outside chance that one of them might recognise something.

'They were not the usual sly or obscene anonymous notes,' Housey said. 'They were blunt and menacing. The first one said, "I'm going to come into your enchanted dream world and make it a nightmare. I'll be thinking about you as you read this. I may even be watching." And it was signed Incubus. Sally was terrified. She went and looked up the word. The encyclopaedia told her that an incubus was an evil spirit supposed to descend on sleeping persons and oppress them like a nightmare. That really scared her, the concept of it. She had to be sedated. Her husband went straight out and hired three security guards to patrol the grounds.'

The second note described to Sally the interior of her bedroom, and rounded off with a promise that she would be martyred in there – 'or by the pool if it's a warm night.'

The content of the notes became more and more ominous and the threats hardened into detail: two days before Sally was finally taken from her bedroom and killed, she was told that every one of her 'available openings' would be filled, and she would perish in an agonising silence.

'The notes were gothic, psychopathic masterpieces,' Housey said. 'The cruelty was calculated and it was carefully graded. But in spite of the persistence of the campaign, and the escalation in the threats, and Sally's mounting fear – her *terror* – neither her husband nor the police really believed anything would come of the threats. The feeling was that in time the incubus, whoever he was, would move on and start scaring some other woman for a change.'

The three security guards immediately came under suspicion, if not principally for the crime then for complicity, because on the night Sally Wimbush was murdered all three were away from their posts without permission. Their story was that they had accidentally managed to lock themselves in the basement locker room where they changed their clothes. The place was heavily soundproofed and no one could hear their calls.

'It is true that in the morning, when the police opened the locker room, all three men were in there, bleary and unshaven,' Housey said. 'There was also a quantity of cocaine and a lot of alcohol. After the guards had passed the forensic tests, it was clear they were no more than a shiftless trio of con-men who should have been stuck in jail for misrepresenting their credentials. But they weren't killers, and they weren't in the pay of killers. They had been sitting around getting stoned, which was probably a regular event, and somebody had locked them in.'

The man who killed Sally, the police realised, was well informed about her domestic arrangements, even down to the details of her bedroom decor and the fact that her guards were rarely ever on patrol. Domestic staff were screened and all delivery people who regularly visited the Wimbush house were checked. The investigations were exhaustive, but the police found no one who could be considered even remotely likely to be involved in a bizarre premeditated murder.

'Meanwhile, though, the forensic medical crowd were aiming to make a case of their own,' Housey said. 'The body of Sally Wimbush was subjected to incredibly thorough examination. Killers, sex killers in particular, leave traces of themselves on and in their victims, and any forensic pathologist worth his hire will want very badly to translate those traces into the identity of the murderer.'

The senior pathologist, Stewart Hornby, confided to Housey early on in the investigation that he knew, after seeing some of the notes Sally had received, that they were going to have a hard time tracking down this killer. 'He said we were trailing a perfectionist, somebody who likes to take his time over details and never acts on impulse. People like that are fewer than we realise, and I had to agree, a methodical, thoughtful man or woman, someone who can foresee angles and accommodate them in the plans, makes a terribly hard criminal to catch.'

Semen samples were absent; smears of lubricant showed that the attacker had used a condom. Dr Hornby decided to swab for saliva, which can sometimes be as incriminating as a semen sample. While running an ultra-violet lamp over the body to show up any hidden marks, he had noticed a couple of short, whitish hairs fluorescing amid Sally's own blonde hair. The indication was that these were artificial fibres, but there was a possible bonus – when the fibres were lifted with low-tack adhesive tape, three darker hairs came with them.

'These were hairs which had probably been drawn by static electric action to the fibres before both the fibres and the hairs were transferred to Sally's head,' Housey said. 'It's worth remembering, while we're on the topic, that a victim's own hair can be a gold-mine for clues, because of its static attraction for particles on the clothing and skin of the attacker.'

While the investigation into the murder of Sally Wimbush went ahead, another woman appeared at police headquarters with a note she had found in her mailbox. The handwriting matched that on the Wimbush notes, and so did the paper. The signature, again, was Incubus.

'I have decided to introduce you to misery,' the note said. 'Soon you will wish you had never been born.'

This time the police took the threat seriously and put a round-the-clock guard on the home of the new target, who was called June Lowry. Like Sally Wimbush, she was young, attractive and had married into substantial wealth. Her husband was a successful actors' agent, and June herself was a former television presenter who now worked from home as a publicist for several of her husband's clients.

'This time the police had nothing to blame themselves for,' Housey said. 'They kept a really close watch on June, and as surveillance and protection operations go, that was a good one. But there was a lot of unspoken uneasiness, because they still didn't manage to intercept the notes, and even though there was a constant police presence, they saw nothing suspicious. The notes just seemed to appear by themselves. A couple of times the officers on duty stopped June getting her hands on the notes, but she saw most of them, and they drove her nearly crazy. As before, the threats escalated, the writer described features of June's bedroom and told her that she would die either in there, or out by the pool if it was warm.'

June died in her bedroom. It happened in the early evening as she was changing for dinner. Friends were coming and an active, entertaining evening had been planned to try to divert her for a few hours.

When half an hour had passed and June still hadn't emerged from the bedroom, her husband went to see what was keeping her. He found June sprawled across the bed, naked and obviously dead. Her mouth and throat were packed tight with animal excrement; wooden chopsticks had been driven into her ears, a crystal candlestick was stuck in her vagina, and when Dr Hornby later examined the body, he found a wooden pencil pushed all the way into the anus.

A combination of panic, anger and financial pressure brought about a sweeping raid of bars, coffee shops and bowling alleys in the vicinity of Beverly Hills. The wealthy residents of the area were suddenly terrified, realising that heavy police protection and electrified wire fences around their properties were no guarantee of safety. If Incubus wanted to get somebody, he got her. Something had to be done, and in the wave of raids that went on during the next two days more than 400 men were interviewed.

Inevitably, Housey said, there were strange people among

those interviewed. That would have been the case in any city, but in Los Angeles the percentage of oddities is always high, and of thirty-eight men put on a shortlist of 'questionables', no fewer than six confessed to the Incubus killings.

'They had to be checked out,' Housey said, 'and so did a lot of men who did not admit anything, who in fact made strenuous denials. Extra officers with interviewing skills had to be drafted in, and a team of psychological profilers was flown in from New York. The police were suddenly overstretched, and the burglary rate went up, which brought more calls from more rich people for something effective to be done. None of this did much for police morale, which took a real nose-dive when a plain-clothes officer was caught by a vigilante group as he attacked a teenage girl in an alley at the back of a bar. The press had a wow of a time. The picture they painted was of a city terrorised by a maniacal killer and ineffectively protected by a corrupt police force.'

The officer found molesting the girl had been drunk; he was a known problem, already working under a warning when he was caught. He was a prominent exception among hard-working, law-abiding colleagues, but that made no difference. The entire Los Angeles police force was tainted.

Then there was another murder. The *modus operandi* was the same as in the previous two: the woman was young, attractive and rich; she was raped, had chopsticks pushed into her ears and other objects put into her vagina and anus, and she was suffocated with animal excrement. Detectives searching the bedroom where she died discovered a series of notes like the others.

'It dawned on them now that this Incubus character was probably terrorising several women at the same time,' Housey said, 'and some of them just weren't telling the police. It was a nightmare, the very worst that could happen. Society in these parts felt completely vulnerable, and the rich guys were discovering that no amount of money or influence could protect their wives.'

Dr Hornby, meanwhile, had made some important discoveries. His saliva tests on all three bodies showed traces on the women's shoulders and breasts. This is not an uncommon finding in rape victims, but in each of the three cases the saliva showed traces of the drug phenytoin.

'Also, the foreign hairs found on the first victim, Sally Wimbush, had turned out to be animal hairs, and that really got Hornby going,' Housey said. 'The profile of a hair is a very clear indication of its animal source – human, ape, rodent, cat, dog and so on. Well, these were cat hairs, and Hornby decided he wanted to know what kind of cat.'

Los Angeles is teeming with specialists, and an authority on the anatomy and physiology of cats was soon tracked down and asked if he could determine the breed of cat from its hair. He said that usually he could, and after only a few minutes looking at the specimens he announced that the hairs belonged to a seal-point Siamese. Dr Hornby had no idea if this information would be useful or not, but at least he had followed that line of inquiry as far as he could. He then proceeded to try to do the same with the evidence of phenytoin in the saliva samples.

Pharmacists in Los Angeles dispense phenytoin in fairly large quantities every year. Under the trade name Dilantin it is regularly prescribed as an anti-convulsant to treat epilepsy, and a number of doctors also use it as a partial treatment for migraine. It is taken regularly by several thousand people in the city. Again, Hornby had gone as far as he could with a line of inquiry, although this one had not led as far as he had hoped it might.

The body of the third victim had a bite mark on the shoulder. Hornby called in a forensic ondontologist to advise. Odontology is the scientific study of the structure and diseases of teeth. In recent years, the work of forensic odontologists had been used extensively in the building of prosecution cases where precise identification of individuals had been important. In this case the specialist photographed the bite mark, then submitted the image to computer enhancement.

'The final picture told us nothing about who had killed the woman,' Hornby recorded in his journal, 'but more and more evidence accumulates by the day, and that can be no bad thing.'

A check was made on all breeders and vendors of Siamese cats in the area, but the resulting list of buyers was believed to be incomplete and was, in any case, too long to use as a door-to-door list. Following a newspaper appeal, however, one breeder had something interesting to report.

'One of his customers had had what he called a "funny turn" while he was being shown the various animals for sale. He covered his eyes with both hands and complained that the thin vertical chrome bars on the cages were making him feel faint. He had to be led away and allowed to sit in the darkened waiting room until the dizziness and nausea passed.'

This syndrome, Housey said, is consistent with mild seizures in epileptics, brought about by the dazzle effect of vertical or horizontal stripes. The cat dealer could not recall the name of the client, but he gave a rough description and added that he believed the man bought a seal-point or a chocolate-point Siamese.

Housey said that if the police had been stacking up evidence too, the public might have looked on them more favourably. As things stood, the general feeling was that a highly dangerous psychopath was dancing rings around all those clean-eyed and over-equipped cops.

A fourth murder attempt was botched when the intruder unwittingly set off alarms and a video surveillance system. He was masked and clad in a black tracksuit, and when he grabbed his intended victim – a young married woman living in a well-guarded mansion on the outskirts of Santa Monica – she was conscious of a bad smell, and she had no doubt what it was.

'Dog shit,' she told a police officer. 'When you've had Dobermans and mastiffs and all those other horse-size canines patrolling your grounds for as long as I have, it's not a smell you can easily mistake.'

When the alarms went off and the video started up, the assailant backed away from his target and almost walked into a guard who had come running to the pool area, his gun drawn. Before anyone had time to caution the intruder, or attempt to seize him, he had run for the far wall and leaped up on to it. In another second he was over the wall and gone.

Housey said that the police then had an incredible stroke of luck. 'They were showing video stills of the masked intruder with his handful of dog pooh to traders and social workers and anybody else they could think of around the area of the intended crime. They were trying to jog memories, and it worked. A sports-shop proprietor told them he had sold the tracksuit in the picture. He swore he'd only had two, and one of them had been sent to his son-in-law in Pittsburgh as a birthday gift. The other was sold to a young man whose credit-card details would be in the records somewhere.'

The records turned up the name Jeff Adams, who was listed in the commercial directory as a voice coach. Police visited his premises, keeping the approach low-key and casual, but with a huge concealed back-up – including armed look-outs on the roofs – covering the entire street.

Adams appeared diffident and nervous, a soft-spoken young man who agreed that he did own a black designer tracksuit of the make the police specified, but that he did not have it around at that time for them to examine because it had been borrowed by a friend. He gave the police the name of the friend, and the police excused themselves and left. During the visit they had seen nothing suspicious, nothing outlandish or strange that would have suggested Adams was the kind of man who could plan and carry out the brutal murders of three women.

'He's a wimp,' one officer announced. 'A wimp with a really nice voice.'

The friend alleged to have borrowed the tracksuit, a drama instructor, was sought at the address Adams gave, in the Anaheim district of Los Angeles. It turned out that he really did live there and was home when the police called. But he denied ever borrowing the tracksuit.

'I mean, look at me,' he said, touching his sweater, his slacks. 'This is Armani, my loafers are Gucci. Do I strike you as the kind of person who *borrows* clothes?'

'So why would your friend lie about a thing like that?' a detective asked him.

'How would I know? He lies all the time, that's his major trademark.'

In the meantime, a rooftop surveillance unit, one of three which remained behind to keep an eye on Jeff Adams' movements, saw him leave his apartment carrying a bundle wrapped in brown paper. He was stopped by a mobile patrol as he began pushing the bundle into a trashcan at the side of the street. They asked him to show them what was in the parcel.

Adams hesitated, then opened the paper, explaining that it was the tracksuit the other officers had asked him about. He had suddenly remembered he hadn't loaned it to a friend at all, and he was on his way to the police station to hand it over for whatever tests they wanted to perform.

When it was suggested that it looked more like he was trying to ditch the tracksuit, Adams denied it. He was asked to accompany the police to the station. He refused and had to be picked up and carried into the patrol car.

At the station, questioned by detectives, Adams denied any

knowledge of the Incubus murders. He was a voice coach, he said, a man who taught certain disciplines and who led a quietly disciplined life. He did not demand much of the world apart from a decent living and the peace to go his quiet way. He was clean, he said, that was the main thing in his life, it was his principal ethic; he was an honest, decent man who had never knowingly bent a law in his life.

He was still denying everything an hour later, when officers who had just searched his apartment showed him two bottles of Dilantin they had found in his bathroom, and a boxful of wooden chopsticks identical to those used in the murders. Adams shrugged. Lots of people bought that kind of disposable chopsticks, they were sold in supermarkets all over the city. And yes, he was an epileptic and had to take an anti-convulsive drug for the condition, that was true, but so what? Lots of people were epileptics, it was no crime.

The officers had also brought a pornographic scrapbook from Adams' apartment. It was filled with drawings and photographs of women being humiliated in various obscene ways. Another telling item was a hand-made sticker. It was removed from a brass paperweight in Adams' small office at the back of the studio where he conducted his business. In fluorescent green letters the sticker said 'MAKE THE BITCHES EAT SHIT'.

Adams continued to deny everything. He had only read about the killings, he said, he did not know the details and he did not care about them. He was an ordinary citizen leading an ordinary life and he could not understand how, on the so-called evidence of a tracksuit in a fuzzy photograph, he was being hounded and coerced towards admitting something he had not done and was not capable of doing.

Housey remembered: 'Even when the accumulated evidence was forcibly put to him – when he was challenged about the coincidence of the chopsticks, the obvious indication that he was interested in the kinks that had been performed on the dead women, the reference to dog excrement on the sticker, and most damning of all, the presence of his epilepsy drug in the saliva on the bodies – *still* he said he was the innocent victim of some horrendous misunderstanding.'

And then an officer who had remained at Adams' apartment to monitor callers radioed the detectives interrogating the suspect. While the officer had been sitting there in the kitchen, a cat had let itself in through a high window flap and helped itself to food from a bowl on the floor by the refrigerator. The cat was a seal-point Siamese, and a tag on its collar was engraved with Jeff Adams' name and address.

The suspect was told that on the evidence as it now stood, he would probably be charged with murder before the day was over.

'And then he changed tack,' Housey said. 'He turned the challenge back on to the police. How could they say that it was him on the video? he wanted to know. How could they say he had been at the scene of any of those killings? He had never been apprehended there, all they had was a bunch of clues that looked like a case, but the fact was they could not put him at the scene. A lawyer, he said, would dispute the argument that no one else would have been wearing such a tracksuit at that time and place; he would point out that lots of people use epileptic drugs, that the chopsticks in the case were very common, and that one set of Siamese cat hairs looks pretty much like any other. They had nothing, he told them.'

Without evidence which put him at the scene of at least one of the crimes, it was true that reasonable doubt could be put forward as a valid cause for a jury to dismiss the case. The police knew that, but they tried to play it down. They were still trying when the senior detective on the case had a call from the pathologist, Dr Hornby. 'He advised us to get hold of the gun that had been drawn at the aborted murder attempt,' the detective said. 'The doc had been watching the video over and over, ferreting for clues, and when he had gotten an enhanced copy of the tape he played it back on a huge monitor in the ballistic lab, and he saw the masked suspect's hand strike the barrel of the guard's gun as he turned and ran for the far wall. It was a real square-on tap on the barrel, the kind that might conceivably leave a mark.'

It was an outside chance, but the guard was located and asked if he had cleaned his gun or done anything else to it since the incident with the masked intruder. He said he had fired it twice at a jack-rabbit, but that was all. The rest of the time it had remained in the holster where he kept it.'

The gun was brought into the police laboratory for testing. Incredibly, a forefinger print matching Adams' was found on the barrel.

'And that was just too much to be plain old circumstantial evidence,' Housey said. 'Adams was charged, and because of that solitary print where he smacked the gun, all the other evidence achieved the status it deserved and his guilt shone like the sun.'

Psychiatric evidence put forward at the trial showed that Adams was arguably schizophrenic, and that ever since he had been humiliated at the age of sixteen by a 'rich bitch' at a disco party, he had harboured a festering dislike of privileged women that amounted to a ritualised, fetishistic hatred, a hatred which he had finally acted upon. 'If it hadn't been well-to-do young women,' the psychiatrist told the court, 'it would have been something else. His condition required a focus, something at which he could aim his malevolence.'

Adams went to jail and not to a hospital for the criminally insane, as he had hoped he would.

In the aftermath of the case, the police were faced with a deeply uncomfortable truth: no matter how stringent their efforts to defend someone and to stop something bad happening, they had been powerless in the face of one man's determination. In spite of an apparently overwhelming police presence, Jeff Adams had taken the simple precaution of reducing his reflectivity, and in that shadowy state he had actually climbed into the properties where he planned to kill his victims, and roamed around them, familiarising himself with the layout and even small details of the decor and fittings.

'With the first victim, Sally Wimbush, the police could have done a lot more to protect her,' Housey said, 'and that last case was an impulse job, Adams admitted that – if it hadn't been, they would probably never have caught him.

'But in the case of June Lowry, the police were thick on the ground. They did all any police presence could do to protect the woman, short of shadowing her every move, yet it emerged that Adams did reconnaissance on the place not just once but three times, and then hc got into the house right under the noses of the police and tortured the woman to death in her own bedroom. The fact is that Adams was more determined than they were. The law was up against a madman's will to succeed, so they stood very little chance of winning. It was a stark truth to learn, and it's one that still stands.'

Talking to the prosecution's psychiatrist after the trial, Adams put it his own way: 'My focus was sharper than anybody clse's,' he said. 'So I got to do what I wanted.'

Conflict

There is a widespread notion that scientists move and work on a plane devoid of passion, dispute or doubt, that the world of scientific investigation is one of harmony and wholesale agreement, and that its findings are absolute truths.

'The man in the white coat,' said a pharmacologist, 'is often depicted as the aloof, all-knowing, condescending nemesis of ignorance and superstition. He is a sexless, emotionless know-all, the very opposite of the bickering, back-biting, jealous, vicious and ultimately insecure characters I've come across on my journey through the wonderful world of science.'

Forensic science was first popularised in Britain during the sixties in a television series called *The Expert*, in which Marius Goring, playing the omniscient hero who never got a speck on his white coat, planted the notion of scientific infallibility in millions of heads, week after week. In more recent times, forensic science has taken a comparative battering as it has been revealed that its practitioners, in certain cases, have done serious harm to the course of justice.

Among other cases, that of the Birmingham Six did much to damage the reputation of forensic science in Britain. Twenty-two people died in the bombing of two Birmingham pubs in November 1974. The police moved quickly and picked up several suspects within a couple of hours. In due course six Irishmen were convicted of the bombings and were given long prison sentences.

At the trial, confessions by four of the six men were supported by chemical tests which showed that two of them, Patrick Hill and Billy Power, had been handling explosives just before they were arrested. The six men's third appeal against their conviction hinged on independent forensic evidence proving that traces of soap or cigarette smoke could have produced the same positive test results. This testimony, together with the revelation that certain other evidence had been withheld at the first trial, resulted in the Birmingham Six being declared innocent and set free in 1991, after spending seventeen years in prison.

Cases like that are certainly rare, and the greater part of all forensic scientific work is conducted under conditions of tight supervision and strict adherence to guidelines, and results are checked and double-checked.

'The problem arises when fixed ideas and old-fashioned thinking get in the way of objectivity,' said a forensic pathologist. 'In this profession, sad to say, there are people who adhere to theories and techniques that were dead before they were born. There aren't too many of them, and they're not men and women in positions of particular power within the profession – for the most part they work at local level, investigating suspicious deaths, but they manage to do their share of damage to the reputation of the profession. An example of woolly, old-fangled thinking is the way some pathologists test the lungs of dead babies to decide whether they were born alive.'

For many years the so-called 'hydrostatic test' was used to determine whether infant lungs had ever breathed air. The lungs were cut into small pieces, which were then dropped in water. If they floated, that was taken as a sign that the child had once been alive outside of the mother. If they sank, it meant that the child had never been alive at all.

'Thoroughgoing rubbish,' said the pathologist. 'The practice is unscientific, it's backward in its theory, and it takes no account of research that has gone forward for the greater part of this century.'

Some doctors still believe in the hydrostatic test and use it to obtain 'proof' of a live birth. In the face of the fact that it was proved long ago that even a tiny degree of decomposition will make lungs and lung fragments float, the traditionalists responded by adding a stage to the procedure whereby they sandwich the lung between sheets of paper and step on it to expel what is called 'additional gas', the gas produced by putrefactive change. It was argued, without proof, that the microscopic globules of breathed air trapped in the fine tissue of a baby's lung cannot be driven out by stepping on it, and will therefore stay behind after the new preliminary stage to give an indication that the lung once drew breath into a live baby.

Polson and Gee's *Essentials of Forensic Medicine*, published in 1973, makes this curt statement about the hydrostatic test:

> The test was suspect in 1900 and requires no detailed discussion, because it is now known to have no value.

'But that makes no difference to those who still swear by dark-age forensic techniques,' said the pathologist. 'All the way along the line of procedures that are used to make the various determinations expected of a forensic pathologist, there are dozens of outmoded and dangerously misleading techniques still embedded, still being used by people from a generation which believed everything it was told and doesn't believe in submitting its thought processes to the influence of any kind of change.'

The blinkered approach, the stubborn loyalty to outmoded principles, would not seem to be an ideal credential for anyone whose job is to determine causes of death, or to give opinions about events surrounding deaths on which the police might be required to act. Yet one such man, Harvey Newton, was an admired medical examiner in an area of southern California until his death in 1987. Colleagues engaged in forensic work for neighbouring police administrations knew of the doctor's faults, but at least one admitted that powerful loyalty, most of it induced by the man's 'likeable' nature, kept them from voicing any criticism throughout his long career. One young doctor, however, did complain, and for his pains he was told in various official and semi-official ways to mind his own business.

'I'm a medical examiner, a competent one I think, and in the early days of my appointment my work often brought me into contact with Dr Newton. Some of the blunders I witnessed nearly made me scream, but a lot of that was to do with the natural arrogance of my youth. Anyhow, the thing about Newton that saved him so often was that he was good in court. He was a smart talker so he made an effective witness.'

The young medical examiner, whose name is Lou, first met Dr Newton when they went together to the scene of a sudden death. The deceased was a young woman in her early twenties. She was curled up on her side on the bed, fully clothed, and had the appearance of being peacefully asleep. Beside her, on the bedside table, was a box which contained a vaginal douche syringe. This is not an uncommon finding, but it is one which nevertheless requires objective investigation.

'Dr Newton took in the scene with some wise chin-rubbing and the occasional knowing nod of the head,' Lou said. 'He decided it was a classic case of pulmonary embolism. She had used the syringe to try to abort herself, he fancied. Then she had put herself right, tidied her clothes, and put things away. Then she had begun to feel strange and had laid down on the bed. That was when the embolism struck her, according to Dr Newton. A truly classic case, he said.'

Dr Newton had voiced his hypothesis not only to Lou, who was then the very junior medical examiner, but to several medical auxiliaries and a couple of police officers. They had all listened respectfully. Then a forensic investigation team arrived, and with them came the senior medical examiner for the region, who had been in the area and was interested in looking at the case.

'I stepped outside,' said Lou, 'because I had a feeling my presence was kind of extraneous, but old Newton stayed in there, and out in the hallway we could hear him repeating his theory to the big chief. Well, it went kind of quiet after that, then Dr Newton came out, nodded curtly to myself and the cops, and left. A few minutes later the senior medical examiner came to the door and asked me if I'd care to look at the body, just to supplement my experience of these sudden deaths. When I went into the bedroom, the chief's assistant was tagging a bottle of capsules. They were barbiturates, the chief told me. He said the girl had killed herself with them – she'd taken so many her mouth was full of half-dissolved capsules.'

On another memorable occasion Dr Newton declared that in his view, a deceased person had been dead for no longer than ten hours. The timing was very important, because it would put certain people near the scene of the death, while others would not have been there at all.

'I saw that body at the same time as Dr Newton did,' Lou said. 'It was lying naked in a bedroom in what was an average spring temperature. There was a green tinge over the dead man's right iliac fossa. I detected a sweetish smell, and rigor mortis was wearing off. Everything told me that the man had been dead for about two days, possibly longer. But Dr Newton told me I'd got that way wrong. He even told me that when it came to mature evaluations of forensic work, he had an instinct for such things, and he certainly knew all a man needed to know about times of death.'

Once Dr Newton visited a house where a man and his wife had both been found dead. The man, an alcoholic, was on the floor, the wife was in a chair by the fireside. A bottle of phenobarbitone tablets lay on a side table, half empty. Dr Newton had told the police accompanying him that he could see at a glance what had happened. His expert opinion was captured on the tape-recorder he used for making verbal notes at the scenes of crimes.

'We have this man's history of chronic drinking and violence, his wife's own record of having to rescue him from the police cells and drag him out of gutters and brawls. A time comes when all that gets to be too much. I think if we look around the place we'll find a note from the wife, and I think we'll find she drugged her husband's drink with her nerve medicine, then when she realised he was dead and the horror of her actions hit home, she took an overdose herself.' A policeman recalled that Dr Newton winked knowingly at that point. 'A lot of people, perhaps lacking adequate experience of these cases, would dismiss this as a suicide pact.'

Then the forensic team arrived and the doctor stopped theorising and set to work. As soon as he moved the body of the woman an interesting feature came to light. There was a kitchen knife sticking out of the side of her chest, concealed until then by her arm.

'By all accounts, Newton wasn't daunted by that,' Lou said. 'He just repeated his theory, but shifted a few of the facts around until it sounded like he had predicted this very scenario, without the detail of the knife. The husband had killed his wife, according to the latest version, and then, realising what he had done in his drunken stupor, he had swallowed a quantity of her tablets and put himself at a proper distance from his miserable life.'

And then a police officer turned over the man on the floor and found a knife sticking out of him, too. Underneath where he had lain, there was a small pool of dried blood.

'I was told Newton's face was marvellous to behold,' Lou said. 'And when they eventually held autopsies on the bodies, neither one had any barbiturate inside them. The tablets were an incidental presence and nothing to do with the crime. The couple had been murdered, of course, and three weeks later two local kids were charged. They had committed the murders for a bet.'

Another case of Dr Newton's which Lou will never forget concerned a child's body which was taken to a morgue as a suspected cot death. She was eighteen months old, well fed and clean. Lou arrived shortly after a medical team had tried to revive the child and failed. The body was taken to the morgue by ambulance and Lou went into the office to make out an incident report. Dr Newton was there, writing up his autopsy notes. Without being asked, he looked at the child's body and told Lou that this case was exactly as the parents claimed – the little girl had simply died in her sleep, the way that many children do. He added that such deaths had a certain appearance which you learned to detect after a few years.

'When I looked at the body in the strong mortuary light I had other ideas,' Lou said. 'The child had bruises on her arms and there was a swelling on the back of her head. Then I palpated the abdomen and it was distended and spongy. I mentioned this to Dr Newton. He said he'd noticed the abdomen, too, but in his view the swelling and the pulpy feel were the early stages of decomposition. This, incredibly, in a child which had been dead only a few hours.'

A family doctor refused to issue a death certificate and an autopsy was ordered by the district attorney. The examination of the child's body showed that she had been beaten to death. Her abdomen was filled with blood from a sheared liver.

'Newton actually had the nerve to tell me, all steady-eyed and sure of himself, that he thought the pathologist doing the autopsy had made a mistake about the abdomen,' Lou said.

He says there were times when he could have believed Dr Newton had received no medical training at all. Yet there he was, a respected part of the justice system, with years of official decisions on his record.

'I really hate to think about how badly he must have gone wrong over the years,' Lou said, 'or how often.'

There have been some classic conflicts among British forensic scientists, and again it has been pathologists who have often been especially forceful in their condemnation of each other: Sir Sydney Smith's account of Sir Bernard Spilsbury's shortcomings is particularly memorable.

David Howatt, a forensic pathologist from Aberdeen, recalled two older men who bedevilled his early years in the profession. At that time – he was talking about the mid to late 1930s – a young man was automatically assumed to know very little when his knowledge was compared to that of an older man in the same field. It was not just a tiny quirk of the profession, Howatt emphasised, it was a persistent pain which he sometimes thought would never end.

'My opinions and judgements were always being undermined by men riven with jealousy, old men scared I would try to bring in some fancy new techniques that they would be forced to learn. If they hated anything, it was the idea of change. Especially if change was going to mean the abandonment of some precious and probably useless old procedure.'

Howatt, now retired, is a gold-mine of stories about the triumphs of forensic science in its early days, but he particularly likes to talk about the 'ruffian scientists' he has encountered, many of them famous in their time and noted for contributions to justice and to man's understanding of the wellsprings of crime. 'If crime were punishable at all its levels, half those old men would have been put away for life.'

Howatt recalled the professor of forensic medicine who taught his students that if they could not detect a cause of death, even after the most thorough examination of the corpse, then the cause could be ascribed to *status lymphaticus*. 'Long after the forensic world at large had stopped using that embarrassing evasion, that outright confession of ignorance,' Howatt said, 'this particular old gent was still peddling it as a valid and indeed respectable conclusion for a forensic pathologist to reach. But it's really only a suppositional judgement which hardly anybody nowadays finds defensible as a cause of death. It was an extremely fashionable cause between 1900 and 1950, roughly, and it came in handy as an explanation of certain sudden deaths for which no real cause could be found, not even by the brightest pathologists.'

At puberty, the thymus gland in the human chest usually shrinks and becomes inactive, but in some people it continues to grow. Sometimes there are other unusual internal features such as bigger than average lymph glands, and sometimes major blood vessels such as the aorta are underdeveloped. 'It was once believed that people in this condition, especially young adults, were especially prone to sudden death from very trivial causes,' Howatt said, 'and occasionally it would take no more than a bump in the wrong place, at the wrong time, to kill them. These deaths left no sign that was visible at autopsy, and the condition was often mixed up with something called vagal inhibition, which is another rather questionable cause of death.'

Following lengthy debate in the medical press, the condition of *status lymphaticus* was put forward less and less often as a cause, or a contributing cause, in cases of unexplained sudden death in the young. It is still thought possible that some people with large, active thymus glands and narrowed aortas are prone to sudden death from trivial causes, but in many cases proving a link would be impossible. *Status lymphaticus* was never scientifically formulated, and it was a negative finding: when it was entered as a cause of death there was no need to show its presence, since an absence of any other signs was taken to be one of the proofs that *status lymphaticus* was the cause of death. 'It probably doesn't exist as a condition,' Howatt said. 'It was a handy cover-up for the gaps in scientific knowledge, that's all.'

Nevertheless, as recently as the mid-1960s, *status lymphaticus* was still being put down as the cause of death on many death certificates. They were written by men and women whose kind still exist today, Howatt says. 'They're people who believe a doctor should show, above all else, consistency in his approach to his craft, and the way to do that is to refuse to learn anything new, and to stave off change at all costs.'

Many such people are still making important decisions in Britain today, he says. 'They help put together prosecution cases for the police and they pass along opinions which are patent baloney, but they are delivered in marvellously resonant and self-assured voices, so they're bound to be right. Nothing turns a policeman's head more rapidly than being patronised by somebody who speaks posh.'

The troglodytes, as Howatt calls them, have a tendency to see themselves as the guardians of something sacred, rather than as practitioners of a craft that is steadily changing. 'They cling grimly to all the bunkum they picked up a hundred years ago, and they don't want to hear about stuff that came along after that. It's disgusting behaviour, but it smacks of traditionalism, and as long as that's a virtue, these ghastly people will be around.'

In a case to which Howatt was called shortly before his retirement, he was asked by the police to render a second opinion on an apparent murder. 'They said it would help strengthen their case. What they wanted was not a second opinion, but another opinion just like the first.' Howatt read the existing paperwork on the case, and found himself intrigued. The pathologist who had first been brought in had already examined the victim, a woman in her thirties, and pronounced at length on her injuries and his theories about what might have happened.

'He was one of the school of dinosaurs I've alluded to,' Howatt said, 'a man from London bristling with honours and opinions based on nothing more than longstanding prejudice. And if I can digress for a minute, I have to say that a lot of the trouble is that forensic science, or certain areas of forensic science, have never been submitted to objective evaluation. Somebody or some committee with a clear scientific mind, and no loyalties within the trade, should be appointed to test the old 'truths' and see if they're worth anything.

'Who says certain things are true and other things are not? In forensic pathology, the answer in a lot of cases is the same kind of person who decides that a daub on a bit of plywood was made by Picasso and is therefore worth a fortune. His opinion is everything – there is no other way to get an evaluation.

'So, anyway, here I am, confronted with the full hauteur of this gifted man's opinion. Because I did a lot of my work in America, I am not generally considered to have the professional breeding that entitles me to contradict such men. But what the hell, it's fun, and when I get to point out they've made a big mistake, it's the purest joy.'

The dead woman, according to the pathologist from London, had been fatally stabbed through the chest during the commission of a burglary by a person or persons unknown. The absence of blood on the body and at the scene generally was a clear indication of severe surgical shock at the moment the point of the knife touched the pericardium (the membranous sac enclosing the heart). The victim, in the view of the man from London, had died of abrupt shock at the invasion of cold steel into her body.

'And then, honest to God I could hardly believe my eyes,' Howatt said, 'I saw he had written, "This is a reflexive effect akin to the well-documented condition of *status lymphaticus*." I thought I was dreaming. I mean, what part of fairyland did this old goat think he was living in? As a matter of interest, by the way, the stuff about severe surgical shock and all the rest of it was bunkum, too. If the woman had died of a cardio-inhibition that he didn't understand, then why not say so? I know why he didn't, of course – he didn't want it to look as if there were things he didn't know.'

When the time came for the post-mortem examination, both pathologists were present and a gross-anatomy techni-cian was on hand to perform the dissection while the doctors took notes.

'Before the cutting began,' Howatt said, 'I had a look at the stab wound, and again I had this vision of a self-deluded old soul dwelling in the misty reaches of unreality. The wound had no blood at its perimeter, its edges showed no trace of bleeding, and there was no hint of a bruise on the wound. In other words, there had been no blood present within the tissues when the knife was stuck in the woman. And that meant, simply, that she was dead before she was stabbed. I pointed this out to the learned one, but he mumbled something about occult vascularity and ordered the technician to get cutting. I told him to stop until a photograph of the wound could be taken. I didn't want that evidence vanishing in a hail of further cuts made by the technician. When the picture was taken, we went ahead.'

The woman had died of natural causes. The internal findings left no doubt that her life had been ended by a major blood clot in her lung. It was later established that her son, visiting her home and finding her dead, had staged the apparent murder and then ransacked the place, stealing her savings and other valuables.

Following the post-mortem, when the cause of death was agreed upon, the older pathologist left the dissection room without another word. When Howatt emerged he had already left the mortuary and was on his way to the railway station to return to London. 'He later complained to my employing authority, in writing, that he had been obstructed throughout the examination by my spurious theorising and my hectoring approach, which did not befit a representative of the medico-legal profession.'

Howatt's favourite story about ungifted men parading as experts went back to the late fifties, when he was working in New York and was hired by an insurance company to undertake a second-opinion autopsy on the body of a young man for the purposes of determining a cause of death.

'Before I got to the venue I had a telephone call from the pathologist who had carried out the first autopsy, to tell me, in effect, that he had the benefit of many years of checking for this condition – he had certified the cause of death as a myocardial occlusion. He hoped I would not be swayed in my judgement by any pressure from parties who might stand to gain from a second opinion that did not concur with the first one. I told him not to worry, I would call it exactly as I saw it.'

Before Howatt began the examination, he was told by a lawyer that the first pathologist was a notorious drunk who held his job through influence in spite of having no talent left. This was the real reason an out-of-town forensic man had been called in for a second opinion – a very large insurance settlement hung on this case, so they wanted a cause of death they could believe, whatever it might be.

'Well, a second-opinion autopsy is a strange thing,' Howatt said, 'because you're opening up a body that's already been opened, and the organs have all been pre-chopped, and for the

235

most part they're not where they belong – the kidneys, for instance, are often packed in wet newspaper and the package is shaped to fit inside the head, because it has weight and stops the empty head bobbing around in the coffin when it's moved. The brain, of course, can't be put back in the head after the examination, because it's chopped to mush and would seep out through the sawed skull and incision in the scalp.'

The various conventions adopted in the reconstitution of a body mean that only pathologists well practised in second-opinion work can usually find their way around the pot-pourri of chopped and sliced organs packed into the abdominal cavity. 'Anyway, you get the picture, it's a bit strange, you have to dig around to find what you need in order to conduct your examination.'

But in this case Howatt could find nothing that suited his needs. Everything, even allowing for the fact that it was chopped and sliced, and out of its original location, looked wrong.

'And then I found a uterus, connected to a plump pair of ovaries,' Howatt said. 'I looked at the young doctor assisting me. He shrugged. So did I. And then we laughed for about five solid minutes, doing it mainly through our noses so that the people in the anteroom wouldn't hear.

'The man who carried out the first autopsy had managed somehow to get the wrong set of insides back into the body. The real innards for this dead young man were stitched up inside a young woman's body somewhere. It was probably buried by then, or perhaps cremated. I never did find out.'

Index